WITH**DRAWN**

UTSA LIBRARIES

THE
SPIRIT
OF THE
TIMES

Amusements in
Nineteenth-Century
Baltimore, Norfolk,
and Richmond

PATRICIA C. CLICK

University Press of Virginia
Charlottesville

THE UNIVERSITY PRESS OF VIRGINIA
Copyright © 1989 by the Rector and Visitors
of the University of Virginia
First published 1989

Library of Congress Cataloging-in-Publication Data
Click, Patricia Catherine.
The spirit of the times : amusements in nineteenth-century
Baltimore, Norfolk, and Richmond / Patricia C. Click.
   p.   cm.
Bibliography: p.
Includes index.
ISBN 0-8139-1220-2
   1. Amusements—Maryland—Baltimore—History—19th century.
2. Amusements—Virginia—Norfolk—History—19th century.
3. Amusements—Virginia—Richmond—History—19th century.
4. Amusements—Social aspects—Southern States—History—19th
century—Case studies.   I. Title.
GV54.M32B344   1989
306'.48—dc19   89-5303
                                                                        CIP

Printed in the United States of America

Library
University of Texas
at San Antonio

To my mother
and the memory
of my father

Contents

Preface

For years social commentators have been declaring that the United States is in the middle of a "leisure revolution." Although concerns about the proper use of leisure are as old as leisure itself, the roots of the current revolution go back to the industrial revolution in the nineteenth century, when work time and leisure time became distinct, quantifiable entities. One consequence of this development was the increase in the number of commercial public amusements.

The so-called amusement problem of the nineteenth century involved issues related to both the content and form of public amusements. What was appropriate amusement? How should aristocratic amusements be modified to fit into a democratic framework? Should amusements and amusement patrons be controlled? If so, who should control? In the following pages I try to sort out some of these issues, to come to a better understanding of nineteenth-century amusements and their significance in everyday life. I am particularly interested in the shifting attitudes toward various amusements and toward amusement itself.

This study began at the University of Virginia in Joseph F. Kett's graduate seminar on nineteenth-century social and cultural history. I thank him for allowing me to dive into untried waters and for his continuing interest and support. It was always comforting to know that there was someone who understood the enormity of my task of trying to piece together information that was often frustratingly elusive. Similarly, I am grateful to Merrill D. Peterson for advice and comments and his ongoing interest in my work.

Numerous scholars have read this manuscript in various stages and forced me to clarify by analysis. I owe thanks to David R. Goldfield and Michael J. McDonald, as well as all those who wished to remain anonymous. They all offered me much good advice.

This book could not have been written without the help of a number of institutions. I owe a great debt to the Interlibrary Loan Division of the

University of Virginia Library. I would also like to thank the staffs of the manuscripts or special collections departments of Perkins Library of Duke University, Wilson Library of the University of North Carolina at Chapel Hill, the University of Virginia Library, Swem Library of the College of William and Mary, the Maryland Historical Society, the Virginia Historical Society, the Virginia State Library, the Sargent Memorial Room of the Norfolk Public Library, and the Valentine Museum. Laura Cox of the Photo Services Department of the Maryland Historical Society, Lacy Dick and Gregg Kimball of the Valentine Museum, and Michael Plunkett and Richard Lindemann of the Special Collections Department of the University of Virginia Library were especially helpful in locating illustrations.

Over the years I have been fortunate to have the friendship and support of a number of interested people. I am especially grateful to Patricia H. Menk for first introducing me to cultural history at Mary Baldwin College, encouraging me to become a historian, and remaining interested in my career. I also wish to thank Melvin Cherno, Thomas E. Hutchinson, Kay Neeley, Gerry Dameron, Michael Wildasin, Colleen Callahan, Claude Chauvigné, and Fleeta Wilkinson for all their kind words and stimulating conversations along the way. Rose and Roger Crickenberger and Steve Early graciously provided lodging and good fellowship for various research trips. The participants at the 1987 conference "Le temps et l'espace du travail et du loisir dans l'Amérique pré-industrielle," sponsored by the Centre de recherches sur l'histoire des Etats-Unis of the Université Paris 7, have been a welcome source of ideas and support this past year.

On the technical side of things, Priscilla Critzer helped with a number of important details in the preparation of the manuscript. Ignatius Kadoma spent hours doublechecking the sources in the bibliography. I thank them both.

Finally, of course, I thank those friends and relatives who always remembered to ask about the progress of "the amusement book." My sister, Carolyn Click, and my mother, Catherine S. Click—who are as happy as I am that this manuscript is finished—were always ready to help with the many details involved in the preparation. I offer them thanks for that, but most of all I thank them for their words of cheer and loving encouragement.

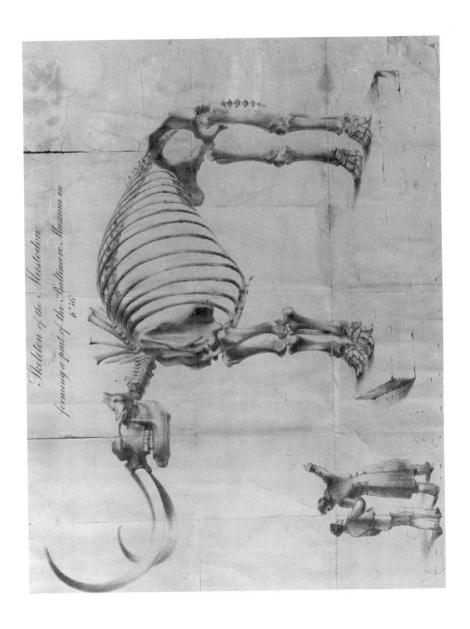

Skeleton of the mastodon at the Baltimore Museum. Lithograph, by Alfred J. Miller, in an 1836 booklet, *A Brief Description of the Skeleton*. (Maryland Historical Society, Baltimore)

PANORAMA!

IN CONNECTION WITH

Mr. GREGORY'S Entertainment

PROFESSOR J. H. FAY

WILL INTRODUCE OVER

 **100**

OF HIS SERIES OF

BEAUTIFUL MOVING AND DISSOLVING

PANORAMIC

VIEWS

COMPRISING

Scenes in the Holy Land,
Europe, Asia, and America;

ALSO, A NUMBER OF

LAUGHABLE COMIC PICTURES!

Forming altogether the most interesting performance ever
introduced for the price of admission.

Come and witness the Show, and TAKE A TRIP AROUND
THE WORD in the space of one hour.

Admission only 25 Cents, to both Shows.

DOORS OPEN AT 7¾ . . PERFORMANCE AT 8¼ P.M.
☞ Front seats reserved for Ladies.   Good order enforced.

Professor J. H. Fay's Panorama. Broadside, Richmond, undated. (Valentine
Museum, Richmond)

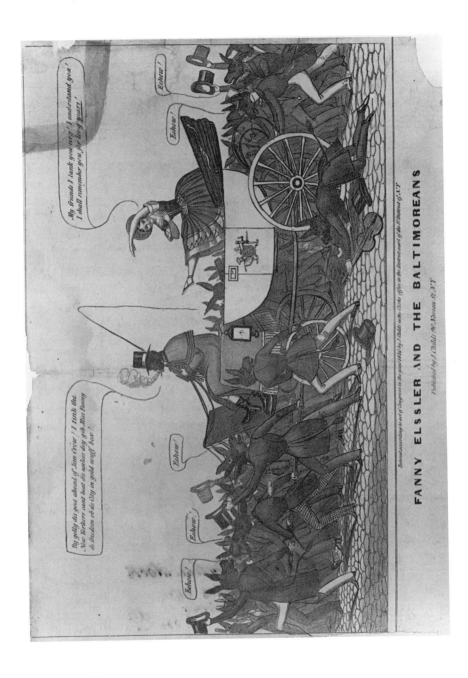

Fanny Elssler and the Baltimoreans, July 1840. Lithograph poking fun at Elsslermania. (Maryland Historical Society, Baltimore)

RULES AND REGULATIONS

OF THE

RICHMOND THEATRE.

WM. L. MAULE, Lessee and Manager.

With a view to preserve the strictest order in the RICHMOND THEATRE, and secure from annoyance visiters desirous of enjoying the performance, the Manager has instructed his officers to see that the following rules are complied with, and he sincerely hopes that the Patrons of the Drama will second his efforts by a strict observance of them:

Gentlemen are most earnestly requested to discontinue wearing their hats in the first tier or dress circle.

Persons in the Theatre will not be permitted to put their feet on the seats, over the backs of the benches or the front of the boxes.

Smoking in any part of the Theatre positively prohibited.

Conversation in a loud tone will not be allowed in any part of the Theatre during the time of performance.

Whooping, hallooing, whistling, or other disorderly noises, positively prohibited.

☞ Any one failing to comply with the above rules, after having been reminded by an officer that he is infringing them, will not only be ejected from the Theatre, but refused admission upon any terms during this season.

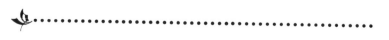

Rules and Regulations of the Richmond Theatre. Broadside, Richmond, ca. 1840. (Valentine Museum, Richmond)

The Great Fight between Tom Hyer and Yankee Sullivan at Still Pond in Kent County. Lithograph, 1849. (Maryland Historical Society, Baltimore)

UTILITARIAN,

BY ECLIPSE,

Too well and favorably known in this

vicinity to need puffing, will stand the ensuing season at Hopewell plantation, 4 miles from Greensboro', on the Withers Landing road, and at
Newbern,---the Season to commence forthwith, and terminate with the
month of July. Terms **$5** the leap, **$10** the season, and **$15** insurance;
in every case **50** cents to the groom. The insurance will be claimed if the
mare is parted from, or can be proved to have been in foal.

For the information of such as may

not have heard of Utilitarian, it may be well to state, that this horse was
carefully bred by his present owner, with reference to useful qualities for
the Harness and the Saddle. The fame of the Eclipses as Carriage horses
is established wherever they have been tried,---while the Roebuck stock,
on his dam side, is equally well known in Virginia, as celebrated goers under the saddle. This horse unites in himself the qualities of both races,
having proved himself a durable and powerful draft horse, and is a smooth
pacer, at the rate of 7 or 8 miles an hour. The amateur breeder of blood-
ed horses will hardly find a better pedigree in the U. S. As a foal getter,
I need only refer the public to his colts on the place where he stands.

PERKINS, Agent
for JOHN D. COCKE.

PEDIGREE.---Utilitarian was gotten by American Eclipse, his dam
Vixen by Roebuck, his gr. dam by the imported Bedford, his g. gr. dam
by imported old Diomed, out of Jeanette, a distinguished runner in Eng-
land, imported to Virginia by the late Col. Hoomes of the Bowling
Green, Va.   J. H. COCKE.
March 9, 1850.

Utilitarian. Broadside, 1850. (Cocke Family Papers [N35-197-E], Special
Collections Department, Manuscripts Division, University of Virginia Library)

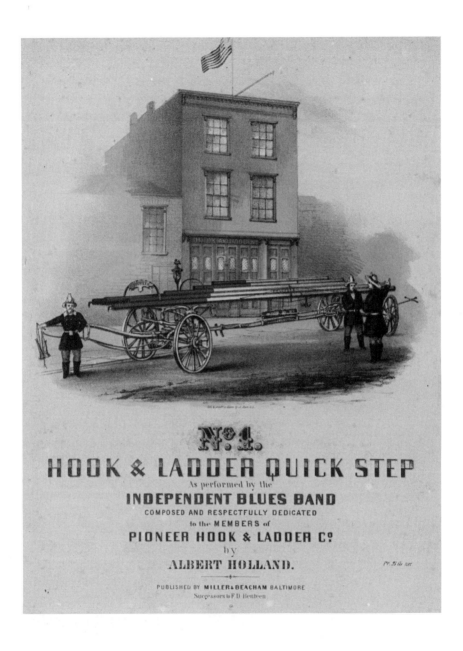

No. 1 Hook & Ladder Quick Step, composed for the official inauguration of the Pioneer Hook & Ladder Company, Baltimore. Lithograph, sheet music cover, ca. 1852. (Maryland Historical Society, Baltimore)

Fair Grounds of the Virginia State Agricultural Society, 1854. Lithograph, Richmond. (Valentine Museum, Richmond)

Heller's World of Wonders! Broadside, Baltimore, 1854. (Maryland Historical Society, Baltimore)

THE BATH ALUM SPRINGS.

Bath Alum Springs. Lithograph, *Harper's New Monthly Magazine,* February 1855.

LAUNCH OF THE UNITED STATES STEAM CORVETTE "RICHMOND," AT NORFOLK, VIRGINIA, ON JANUARY 26, 1860.—[SEE PAGE 90.]

Launch of the U.S. Steam Corvette *Richmond* at Norfolk. Lithograph, *Harper's Weekly*, February 11, 1860. (Special Collections Department, Manuscripts Prints Collection [N35-197-J], University of Virginia Library)

This Celebrated Four Mile Race Horse,

Will stand the ensuing Season, commencing the *First of March*, and ending 15*th July*, at Campbell Court-house, and will be let to mares at $50 the season, to be paid at the end of the season, and $75 insurance, to be paid when the mare is ascertained to be with foal or parted with. One dollar to the Groom in all cases.

Mares from a distance will be furnished with pasturage on the finest grass plats of Orchard, Herds grass and Timothy, gratis, and if preferred, will be fed on grain at 60 cents per day. Every care will be taken to prevent accidents or escapes, but no responsibility assumed in any case. All charges must be paid before the mares are taken away.

PEDIGREE.

RED EYE was by Boston, out of Lucy Long, who was by Imported Priam out of Polly Franklin, who was by Shakspeare, who was by Virginian, he by Sir Archie, and his dam by Shanandoah, and he by Potomac: Polly Franklin's, Dam was by Potomac, and he by Old Diomed, her grand dam by Bedford, g. g. dam by Wildair, g. g. g. dam by Shark, and g. g. g. g. dam by Othello.

DESCRIPTION.

RED EYE is a beautiful Bay, with black main and tail; dark legs, except a little white on his pasterns behind; full sixteen hands high, of superior action; fine bone, and a back and loin not inferior to any horse whatever, combining great beauty and symmetry of form.

☞ The following is an account of his performances on the Turf, from the Spring of 1849, to the Fall of '54, inclusive:

The Performances of the Celebrated Race Horse, Red Eye, on the Turf, from the Spring of 1849, to the Fall of 1854, inclusive.

DATE	AGE	COURSES.	PURSES.	WINNING HORSES.	LOSING HORSES.	Length of Heats.	No Heats	Single Dashes.	Notes.
1849, Spring	3	New Market	S. $100 entrance	Boston Colt	Red Eye and others	1 Mile.	3		a
" "	3	Fairfield	S. $100	Gratis	Red Eye and others	1 "	2		b
1850, "	4	New Market	Proprietor's Purse	Financier	Red Eye	2 "	2		c
" "	4	Fairfield	Citizens' Plate	RED EYE		1 "	2		
" "	4	Broad Rock	Proprietor's Purse	RED EYE	Thirteen of Trump, Dick Earnest	2 "	3		
" Fall	4	" "	Post Stake	Mary Mason	Red Eye	3 "	2		d
1851, Spring	5	" "	Proprietor's Purse	Financier	Red Eye. Time: 3.46—3.47	2 "	2		
" "	5	Fairfield	" "	RED EYE	Financier. Time: 3.44—3.55—3.47	2 "	3		
" "	5	New Market	Jockey Club	RED EYE	Protection	2 "	2		
" "	5	Norfolk Course	" " $500	RED EYE	Financier	3 "	2		
" Fall	5	Fairfield	" " 500	RED EYE	Lady Fairfield, Mary Marsh. Time: 5.45—5.47	3 "	2		
" "	5	Fairfield	" " 400	RED EYE	Virginia Payne, Bloomer, Virginia Rose.	3 "	2		
" "	5	Broad Rock	" " 500	RED EYE	Lady Fairfield, Mary Marsh.	3 "	2		
1852, Spring	6	Norfolk Course	" " 500	RED EYE	Trojan	3 "	2		
" "	6	Broad Rock	" "	RED EYE	Gold Pin, Virginia Payne	2 "	2		
" "	6	New Market	" "	RED EYE	Bazel	3 "	2		
" Fall	6	Fairfield	" " 400	RED EYE	Lady Fairfield, Ben Quarles.	3 "	2		
			" " 600	Gold Pin	Red Eye	3 "	2)		e
			and in st. 500						
	6	Broad Rock	Jockey Club 600	Gold Pin	Red Eye	3 "	2)		
			and in st. 500						
" "	6	New Market	Jockey Club 500	RED EYE	One Eye Joe	2 "	2		
" "	6	Norfolk Course	" " 500	RED EYE	One Eye Joe, Tom Walker	3 "	2		
1853, Spring	7	"	Match, $2,000 forfeit	RED EYE	Gold Pin paid forfeit	4 "	Walked.		
			300						
" "	7	" "	" " 200	RED EYE	Maid of Edgcomb, Florence, White Eye. Time: 3.42	2 "	1	1	
" "	7	" "	Jockey Club 500	RED EYE		3 "	Walked.		
" "	7	New Market	Proprietor's Purse. 250	RED EYE	One Eye Joe	2 "	2		
" "	7	Broad Rock	Jockey Club 400	RED EYE	Lawson	3 "	2		
" "	7	Fairfield	" " 700	RED EYE	Lawson, Maid of Edgcomb, Jeff. Davis.	4 "	2		
" 11th June	7	"	Match, [a side] 2,500	RED EYE	Nina	2 "	3		
" Fall, Septemb'r									
27th	7	"	Match, [a side] 5,000	Nina	Red Eye	2 "	2		
" Fall	7	" "	Jockey Club 500	RED EYE	Lawson	4 "	2		
1854, January	7	Broad Rock	" " 500	RED EYE	Nina, Lawson. Time: 7.46—7.46 |—7.49	4 "	3		f
" "	8	Augusta, Ga.	" " 800	RED EYE	Maid of Edgcomb	4 "	2		g
" February	8	Charleston, S. C.	" " 500	RED EYE		4 "	Walked.		
			800	John Hopkins		3 "	1		
" Spring	8	Broad Rock	" " 800	RED EYE	Red Eye, Florence	3 "	1	1	h
" "	8	New Market	" " 800	RED EYE	Lawson	4 "	2		
" "	8	Fairfield	" " 800	RED EYE	Lawson	4 "	2		
" "	8	Herring Run, Baltimore	" " 1,000	RED EYE	One Eye Joe, Fanny Fern	4 "	3		
" September	8	National, N. Y	" " 1,000	RED EYE	Wild Irishman	2 "	1		i
	8	" "	" " 2,000	RED EYE	Red Eye, Granite, Maid of Orleans, G. Davis, &c.	4 "	3		
" Fall	8	New Market	" " 500	RED EYE	Highlander, One Eye Joe, Rube, Little Flea	4 "	3		
" "	8	Broad Rock	" " 600	RED EYE	One Eye Joe, Nat Blick, Lawson	4 "	3		
" "	8	Fairfield	" " 800	RED EYE	Rube	4 "	2		

NOTES.—(a) Red Eye wouldn't run. (b) Red Eye wouldn't run. (c) Red Eye ran the first mile in the second heat in 1.49,—mud ankle deep. (d) Red Eye bolted in the third mile of the second heat when three or four lengths ahead, and was very near killing both his rider and himself. (e) Red Eye got "off" his foot before the first of three two races; and did not recover until after the race at New Market. (f) Red Eye won this race easily in two straight heats without a "lick," but the purse was awarded to Lawson in consequence of foul riding, in the quarter stretch, by Anderson, (Red Eye's rider,) for which he was publicly expelled from the Course. (g) Red Eye made the best four mile race of three heats ever made in America. (h) Red Eye was sulky and could'nt be made even to walk around the track. (i) Red Eye was only entered here for exercise, to prepare for the great four mile race three days afterwards, which he won in three heats.

☞ RED EYE goes off the turf a winner of 31 out of 43 races; and never has lost a Four Mile Race! He has run in miles 265, and won 225 of them. Can any horse in America show such a record?

RED EYE was exhibited, for the first time, in the Fall of 1855, at the Virginia and North Carolina Agricultural Fair, held at Petersburg, and at the State Fair of Virginia, at Richmond. At the former he received the First Premium of $50, offered for the best thorough-bred Stallion; at the latter he received the first Premium of $50, for the best thorough-bred Stallion, and another Premium of $20, offered for the best Horse of his species, was also awarded him.

☞ His Colts received the First Premium at all the Fairs at which they were exhibited last Fall.

CAMPBELL COURT-HOUSE, Feb. 22nd, 1860.   *John D. Alexander*

From JOHNSON'S Power Press Printing Works, 61 Market Street, Lynchburg, Va.

Red Eye! Broadside, Lynchburg, Va., 1860. (Valentine Museum, Richmond)

The beach at Nags Head, North Carolina, a popular resort of Norfolk residents. Lithograph, *Harper's New Monthly Magazine,* May 1860.

GRAND TRUNK RAILWAY.

Baggage handling at Nags Head, showing the resort's wooden railway for carting belongings from ship to shore. Lithograph, *Harper's New Monthly Magazine*, May 1860.

BLACK HAWK AND POST BOY.

BLACK HAWK will stand at my Stable this season, ending the 1st of July at $30 the season, and 50 cents to the groom. Mares not discharged may be continued till done with, or to the 1st. October, and those not proving in foal will be insured next season for $20 only, in each case payment must be punctual or a Negotiable Note.

DESCRIPTION.

BLACK HAWK is eleven years old, weighs 1085lbs., is 15½ hands high, a glossy black, perfection in form ; his speed when trained at six years old, was 2.44, in a race of six heats of a mile each. He was awarded at the last five Fairs he was at, six prizes, the last at Richmond, last fall was awarded unanimously as the best Quick Draft Horse, $100.

PEDIGREE.

His Dam was a Black Hamiltonian Mare and splendid breeder, and was sired by Hill's famous Black Hawk, he by Sherman, and Sherman by Justin Morgan, who was foaled in 1793, and the founder of the most celebrated stock of Horses in America.

Black Hawk's branch of the Morgan horses is more famous than any or all of them, and the breeder who fails to avail himself of the chance, greatly neglects his interest.

POST BOY.

Will stand at my Stable, at the Cross Roads in the North Garden, and at Mechum's River, dividing his time as may be necessary, till the 1st. of July, at $15 the season, and 50 cents to the groom ; and such Mares as may require it can be continued to him, at my stable till 1st. October, should he not be sold in the mean time.

DESCRIPTION.

POST BOY is 6 years old, nearly 16 hands high, a beautiful Bay, weighs 1130lbs. is a rapid trotter, but was never trained. He was sired by Black Hawk, and shows the size of his first colts, though his dam was a small but fine Post Boy Mare. All that is said of Black Hawk is applicable to Post Boy, and between the two, breeders can find a fit cross on any mares they may likely have.

S. W. FICKLIN.

Belmont, April 1st. 1861.

Black Hawk and Post Boy. Broadside, [Charlottesville, Va.], 1861. (Cocke Family Papers [N35-197-I], Special Collections Department, Manuscripts Division, University of Virginia Library)

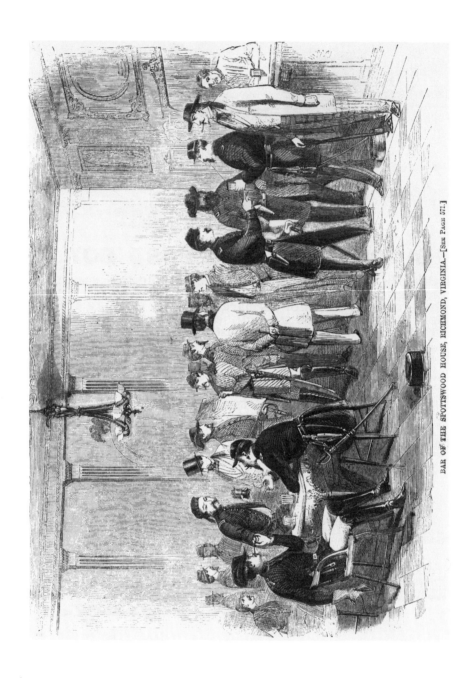

BAR OF THE SPOTSWOOD HOUSE, RICHMOND, VIRGINIA.—[See Page 571.]

Richmond's Spotswood House bar, September 7, 1861. Lithograph, *Harper's Weekly*. (Special Collections Department, Manuscripts Prints Collection [N35-197-K], University of Virginia Library)

Card playing at White Sulphur Springs. Photograph, ca. 1865–70. (Valentine Museum, Richmond)

RICHMOND THEATRE!

OPERATIC MATINEE

FOR THE

BENEFIT

OF THE

Poor of Richmond !

The Committee take great pleasure in announcing, that through the generosity of MAX STRAKOSCH, Director of the

GHIONI & SUSINI

GRAND

ITALIAN OPERA!

They are able to announce for

SATURDAY, April 7, 1866,

At 2 o'clock, an OPERATIC CONCERT, in which all the artists of this celebrated Company will appear in

THE CHOICEST GEMS

From the Operas, introducing scenes in costume.

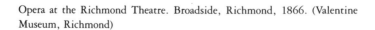

Opera at the Richmond Theatre. Broadside, Richmond, 1866. (Valentine Museum, Richmond)

Concordia Hall in 1866. Lithograph from an unidentified German-language publication. (Maryland Historical Society, Baltimore)

White Sulphur Springs group. General Joseph E. Johnston is standing on the far right, and Custis Lee is seated on the right. Photograph, 1869, reproduced from glass plate. (Valentine Museum, Richmond)

The Hygeia Hotel, Old Point Comfort. Lithograph, advertisement, ca. 1870.
(Special Collections Department, Manuscripts Prints Collection [N35-197-
L], University of Virginia Library)

THE SPIRIT OF THE TIMES

Amusements in Nineteenth-Century Baltimore,

Norfolk, and Richmond

·•·

Introduction

The *Spirit of the Times* was a popular journal that covered leisure activities, primarily sporting events, during the nineteenth century. A study of nineteenth-century amusements suggests that the period did have a special amusement spirit—a spirit that was forged by numerous tensions. First, there was the ongoing tension with respect to the content of amusement. Was the purpose of amusement edification? Or was there justification for secular amusement? In addition, there was the tension between the desire to democratize amusements and the desire to maintain social hierarchy. French visitor Michel Chevalier noticed at least part of this struggle in 1835, when he contrasted Europe's aristocratic amusements with the possibilities in America, noting that democracy was "too much a newcomer in the world to have been able as yet to organize its pleasures and its amusements." He concluded: "In this matter, then, as in politics, American democracy must create everything anew."[1] What Chevalier did not emphasize was that some people still wished to maintain hierarchy. The conflict between them and those with democratic leanings led to some interesting developments in nineteenth-century amusements.

This study is a look at how these and related tensions shaped nineteenth-century amusements and created "everything anew" in three Southern urban centers of the United States. It focuses on amusements in urban areas because, quite simply, the historical sources, though limited, are still more extensive than those for rural society. In addition, the institutionalization of popular amusements was, for the most part, an urban phenomenon. Theatrical productions and exhibitions, for example, were rare in rural America. The specific loci of the study—Baltimore, Maryland; Norfolk, Virginia; and Richmond, Virginia—were picked because they were alike enough to offer the possibility of generalization but different enough to suggest some distinctions because of size and the composition of their respective populations. It should be noted from the start that, surprisingly, during the period of this study, 1800 to 1870, the overall responses to amusements were almost identical in the three cities. Although unique events or developments—epidemics or Civil War battles, for example—meant short-term alterations in amusement patronage in individual cities, the general pattern was not altered. Likewise, all cities suffered from economic dislocations and depressions during this period, especially in 1819, 1837, and 1857; but they did not greatly curtail the development of the commercial amusement sector.

Concentration on the period from 1800 to 1870 allows the study of attitudes during the antebellum period and their comparison with those prevalent during and shortly after the Civil War. In particular, it enables a test of Dale Somers's hypothesis that the Civil War "wrought few profound changes" in the "uses of leisure time in the South."[2] Indeed, continuity rather than change proved to be the rule in Baltimore, Norfolk, and Richmond. This finding, of course, helps affirm the role of ongoing tensions, rather than short-term events or developments, in shaping amusements and amusement patronage.

The emphasis here is on amusements and values rather than the three cities. Amusements, specific activities that human beings pursue for pleasure and/or edification in their leisure time, are distinguished from the institution of amusement, a more general term. Similarly, amusements are differentiated from leisure, which is a much broader term referring to unobligated time.[3] While amusements were nearly always pursued during periods of leisure, leisure was not always filled with amusements. Recreation, the active involvement of an individual in an activity, and entertainment, which often is more passive (spectatorship), are both considered amusements.

Amusement is a tricky term, especially when used with respect to nineteenth-century leisure activities. Citizens of the Upper South during the early part of the century did not often use the word. When they did, *amusement* was usually preceded by the qualifier "innocent" or justified on educational grounds. During the nineteenth century the word *amusement* underwent a metamorphosis—a shift in connotation that reflects changes in some very basic assumptions about amusements and their place in society. During the early part of the century, amusement was contrasted with recreation. Some people, particularly clergymen, thought that amusements should be avoided because they wasted time; they merely gave pleasure. As Southern minister Thomas Charlton Henry, a Presbyterian, underscored in 1825, man's purpose certainly was not pleasure: "To say that we were sent into the world merely to enjoy ourselves in its pleasures, is to utter the language of the grossest sensuality."[4]

Recreation, however, was acceptable because it complemented labor. Recreation refreshed and restored workers so that they could return to work and be more productive. "Rational recreation never loses sight of duty," noted Rev. J. T. Crane, a minister in the Methodist Episcopal church. "It teaches us to seek, now and then, a little leisure, that we may be able to labor the harder and longer."[5] This idea remained popular, especially with some of the more conservative clergy, until well into the nineteenth century. Early in the century, amusement promoters, whether of the pleasure gardens, springs, or concerts, labeled their entertainments "recreation" and emphasized the restorative aspects. When the word *amusement* was used, the emphasis was on refreshment, rather than fun. Thus, in 1813 an advertisement for the proposed monthly magazine *Literary Visitor* stated, "To what amusement can attention be directed with more advantage than that which, while it refreshes the body, invigorates the mind?" In Baltimore, Norfolk, and Richmond the word *amusement* was not generally used in newspaper headings for leisure activities until the 1850s.[6]

Clerical attempts to alter the meaning of the word *amusement*—to give it a more positive definition—during the middle of the century suggest the increased interest in amusement. Clergyman Frederic Sawyer's definition is typical of those that broadened the meaning of amusement and gave it more positive attributes: "The name comes from the Latin *musa*, a song, signifying to allure the attention lightly, like a song. Amusements are only one of the thousand classes of aids to pleasure. There is embraced under the head of amusements all those entertainments, diversions, sports, recreations, pastimes, games, and plays, that belong to the light, cheerful, and sportive employments of our powers of body and mind, in distinction from those that are laborious and serious."[7] In 1859 another Presbyterian minister, James Leonard Corning, noted that *amusement* was a better word for expressing "the dividing line between rest and labor" than *recreation*. Corning also observed that the amusement question was a popular topic of discussion. "Call together a dozen Christian people at random," he noted, and they would disagree about what amusements, if any, were "lawful and proper for a Christian."[8]

Arguments over definition were symptomatic of the real issue, which was the acceptability of secular amusements as a proper way to spend leisure time. Noting that she had been "sorely tried" in making a decision to attend an opera, a young Richmond woman summarized the dilemma: "I *cannot* think it wrong—it appears to me, the most innocent, & scientific of enjoyments—but my kinsfolk & acquaintance . . . imagine if you go to the *Theatre,* you are fit for *purgatory* & so, whether to go, or not, I cannot decide—*their opinion* is all that prevents me."[9] A young Baltimore woman indicated that she enjoyed her night at a Baltimore theater and almost died from mirth until she returned home, when her "mother's sad looks soon disquieted" her. To please her mother, she "made the promise of not going again" that season. *"Was that not dutiful?"* she concluded.[10] In Baltimore the Museum Theatre conveniently occupied the same floor as the museum. Conscience-stricken patrons spent a great deal of time visiting the museum. With tongue in cheek, Baltimore historian Jacob Frey reminisced that the patrons "would have been quite shocked had any one intimated that they were ever induced to linger by the attractions of the theatre."[11]

Paradoxically, the tension between competing definitions of amusement was not always reflected in amusement attendance. The theater, for example, enjoyed a general popularity despite clerical attacks. Nevertheless, there was always an undercurrent of justification, seen especially in the numerous editorials supporting drama because it was inspirational. The theater, noted one Baltimore correspondent in 1810, "instructs while it amuses, and conduces much to that grace and elegance of conversation and manners so fascinating in private life."[12] In 1819 another correspondent defended the theater by comparing it to other less innocent amusements:

> We will not fatigue the reader by a formal essay on the moral effects of the stage. It is enough for us to know that those who have youth and spirits and leisure on their side, will go in search of amusements, and that there is no comparison between the refined pleasures of a theatre, and the gross dissipations of the gaming table. Men, too, in the graver professions and pursuits of the world, will seek to refresh their spirits & to unbend themselves. And certainly we know of no source of amusement more exquisite than to sit and listen to the strains of the gigantic genius of Shakespeare.[13]

Trends in amusement patronage and organization suggest that the 1830s and 1840s marked a departure from the past. It was during this period that the number of amusements increased enough to allow patrons some choice. This period was also when amusement promotion got its start. A new group developed—men whose job was primarily the promotion of amusements. Amusements, in effect, were the core of a new industry, which built upon the organizational structure that grew up in the 1830s. Proportionally, there were more amusements that were pure entertainment—amusements that could not be justified on educational grounds. It was also during the 1830s that many of the amusement-related journals were founded. The *American Turf Register* (begun in Baltimore in 1829) and the *Spirit of the Times* had wide followings in Baltimore, Norfolk, and Richmond. In addition, *The Budget of Fun*, which the *Baltimore American* labeled a "sprightly journal," was popular in Baltimore.[14]

By the 1840s and 1850s even the opponents of secular amusements had resigned themselves to the presence of amusements. A Richmond resident, George W. Munford, reflected a fairly common attitude when he observed that it was useless to attempt to prevent amusements, particularly among the young. Munford thought it obvious that "all young people will dance and will have the amusements that suit their age till the end of the world."[15] Baltimore theater manager William B. Wood said much the same thing about the general public:

> The people will not be without amusements of some sort. That all parties, police, philosophers, moralists, and clergy may depend upon. . . . For those who cared for neither negro singers, nor Italian ones, for dancing girls, nor posture women, new resorts have been multiplied in gaming houses, which are now found in every part of every large American city in number, splendor of appointments, and successful result to the manager who carries misery to so many happy homes, entirely transcending all that the growth of our cities, and the depravity incident to cities could make natural.[16]

One obvious indication of the popularity of amusements by the mid-nineteenth century was the number and variety of commercial public amusements that drew popular support. In Baltimore, Norfolk, and Richmond the growth of the amusement sector was noted frequently in the press. Even in 1863, when the Civil War was rampaging around Richmond, the editor of the *Richmond Enquirer* concluded that Richmond was "favored with fun." Residents could choose among burlesque, serious drama, concerts, and comedy.[17] The more adventuresome did not have to look far for a gambling den or even a brothel. Editorial comments both during and after the war suggest the extent of popular support for secular amusements.[18]

Frederic Sawyer had attempted to bolster his argument for a broadened definition of amusement by pointing out the value of social mixing in public amusements, especially "the opportunity it gives the poorer classes to improve their tastes and manners, by observing those above them, whose advantages have been greater."[19] Ironically, by the time Sawyer wrote these words in 1847, the opportunity for mixing among classes was limited in public amusements. Despite the emphasis on democracy, social mixing in amusements decreased during the antebellum period. Looking at how the tension between democracy and hierarchy helped to shape nineteenth-century amusements and attitudes toward amusement requires some discussion of the role of social status and social class. Both terms are problematic—the first because it smacks of relativity, the second because it means different things in different academic disciplines. Rather than regarding class as a strict term that defines rank purely in economic terms, this study employs a more general definition of class, one that defines social strata through a variety of factors such as income, occupation, ancestry, neighborhood, and connections and also incorporates social status. The population is divided into upper, middle, and lower classes, with occasional references to subdivisions such as the upper-middle class. The reason for this is simple; besides facilitating discussion, the general definition is the one most used by those who are the subjects of this study, or at least, those who wrote about class—usually the upper class or the aspiring middle class.[20]

When this study was begun, there were not many other studies of amusements or leisure. Although commercial public amusements in the antebellum period still do not figure prominently in recent scholarship, a number of historians have published studies of leisure and, in the process, have created a new field of historical inquiry dealing with the relationship between leisure and social development. These scholars raise a variety of questions about the changing value of leisure during the era of the United States' industrial development, the role of leisure in defining class and status conflicts, and the extent to which workers created and/or controlled their own leisure pursuits.[21]

While some of the recent studies include discussions of the relationship of particular leisure choices—sports clubs, for example—to social status, most do not cover the changing attitudes toward both particular amusements and the idea of amusement itself. This study is an attempt to do this. More specifically, it is an effort to document the evolution of nineteenth-century amusements and uncover some of the reasons for the acceptance or rejection of certain amusements. The results suggest that despite the democratic rhetoric of the nineteenth century, amusements were stratified, and the ongoing stratification played a role in denoting the relational nature of the various social classes, as well as the acceptance or rejection of particular amusements and the greater acceptance of amusement in general. In contrast to most of the leisure studies, however, this study is not an attempt to relate struggles in the workplace to struggles over control of popular amusements.[22]

The existing secondary material about amusements is very limited in scope—primarily attempts to show the growth or multiplications of amusements. Organized sports have received the best treatment, although often the emphasis has been on a particular sport or on commercialization, rather than on the interaction of sports and society. Thus, in this study secondary studies of amusements were used mostly for background. Histories of Baltimore, Norfolk, and Richmond helped to give a better understanding of the social life in each of these towns. Secondary sociological studies of such things as leisure theory, social stratification, and agency enhanced the overall historical perspective.

Newspapers, particularly the *Baltimore American and Commercial Daily Advertiser,* the *Norfolk and Portsmouth Herald,* the *Norfolk Virginian,* the *Richmond Enquirer,* and the *Richmond Whig* were helpful in gaining a feel for what was occurring in the cities. Editorial comments were enlightening, though infrequent, while advertisements of coming events were very useful. Letters and diaries from people who lived in the three cities were good sources of accounts of particular events and descriptions of crowds, as well as indices of changing attitudes.

The problem with such manuscript material is, of course, related to the selective nature of what is extant. There is very little written from the viewpoint of the poorer white or the black, both slave and free.

Introduction

Travel accounts compensate to a small extent by offering contemporary descriptions of the cities, the people in general, and amusement crowds in particular. Still, drawing conclusions about the amusement habits of the lower-class and black citizens is difficult. Given these limitations, this study attempts to sketch an introductory picture of amusement participation in the three cities in hopes of understanding how amusements reflected society in Baltimore, Norfolk, and Richmond during the first half of the nineteenth century. Developments were not always straightforward, and ambiguities and paradoxes abound. That, of course, is what makes the story so intriguing.

Chapter one, an overview of the three cities during the antebellum period, presents some of the issues that will be developed in the pages that follow. Chapters two through six discuss some of the popular amusements in nineteenth-century Baltimore, Norfolk, and Richmond, concentrating on the period from 1800 to 1870. Here the focus is on the changes in the specific amusement forms themselves, as well as changes in the types and levels of participation. Because it would be impossible to cover every single amusement in detail, this study concentrates on amusements that involved some sort of public social intercourse and expenditures for admission or participation. Thus, the emphasis is on amusements such as exhibitions, lectures, the theater, gaming, horse racing, club memberships, and sojourns at resorts, rather than solitary ventures such as hunting, fishing, or needlework. Although public executions are discussed in conjunction with exhibitions, generally the study does not include free public entertainments such as street entertainment and parades. The conclusion offers some final thoughts about the significance of some of the important developments in Baltimore, Norfolk, and Richmond.

Chapter One

...

The Setting: Baltimore, Norfolk, and Richmond

... **S**peaking at Chautauqua in 1880, President James A. Garfield divided the struggle of the human race into two chapters. First, there was the "fight to get leisure." Then came "the fight of civilization—what shall we do with our leisure when we get it?"[1] The latter part of the struggle was still in progress during the nineteenth century, when Americans— particularly urban Americans—began to consider some fundamental questions about the form and content of popular amusements. Many continued to fear the consequences of too much idleness, but they no longer automatically assumed that amusement and idleness were one. The process of creating popular amusements that were uniquely American reflected prevalent values and social concerns. In addition, amusement patronage and support mirrored changing expectations about the role of amusement in social life.

Despite their differences, Baltimore, Norfolk, and Richmond exhibited a remarkable similarity with respect to attitudes toward amusements. Thus, it is possible to outline general trends that illustrate the transformation in expectations about amusement. Even as the century opened, the three cities were large enough to support a variety of amusements. All three were busy ports and commercial centers. Consequently, they had heterogeneous populations, which by mid-century included large numbers of blacks (free and slave), as well as recent immigrants, especially Germans, Irish, and Jews. Traveling thespians, lecturers, singers, and other entertainments visited the cities, which were included in the major North-South entertainment circuit.[2]

Each city, however, had its distinctive characteristics. The most obvious difference among the three was size, as shown in the population figures in Table 1. Baltimore grew from a little over 26,500 in 1800 to

Table 1. Populations of Baltimore, Norfolk, and Richmond, 1800–1870

| | Baltimore | | | Norfolk | | | Richmond | | |
	Total	Free black	Slave	Total	Free black	Slave	Total	Free black	Slave
1800	26,514	2,771	2,843	7,700	352	2,724	5,737	607	2,293
1810	35,583	3,973	3,713	9,193	592	3,825	9,735	1,189	3,748
1820	62,738	10,326	4,377	8,478	599	3,261	12,067	1,235	4,387
1830	80,625	14,790	4,323	9,816	928	3,757	16,060	1,960	6,345
1840	102,313	17,967	3,199	10,920	1,026	3,709	20,153	1,926	7,509
1850	169,054	25,442	2,946	14,326	956	4,295	27,570	2,369	9,927
1860	212,418	25,680	2,218	14,620	1,946	3,284	37,910	2,576	11,699
1870	267,354			19,229			51,038		

Source: Federal Census Reports for 1800–1870; Richard Wade, *Slavery in the Cities: The South, 1820–1860* (New York, 1967), pp. 328–30.

more than 267,000 in 1870. Norfolk was much smaller and grew at a slower rate; its population of 7,700 in 1800 had grown to around 19,000 by 1870. Richmond was smaller than Norfolk in 1800—approximately 5,700—but grew more rapidly, to over 51,000 by 1870.

Located where the Patapsco River flows into the upper Chesapeake Bay, Baltimore was the major port and commercial center of the Middle Atlantic; during the first half of the nineteenth century, the port, in fact, was the third largest in the United States. Baltimore was also a manufacturing center, heavily involved in shipbuilding and cotton manufactures. By the 1820s manufacturing and commerce supported each other; trade centered on home-processed and manufactured materials, rather than reexports. Most settlement was centralized around and below the center market and on Fells Point, known locally as the Point. Approximately 60 of the city's 104 inns, taverns, and coffeehouses were located in this area.[3]

Arriving by steamer in the antebellum period, visitors would have been impressed by the large warehouses and shipbuilding facilities, as well as the cosmopolitan nature of the work force. At the same time, guests might have been amused to see boys skinnydipping near the pilings off the shipyards. They would have noticed the developing zone of industry in the area between Federal Hill and the inner harbor. Moving to the center of the city, they would have seen the Washington

The Spirit of the Times

Monument as well as the other large memorials that gave Baltimore the nickname "the Monumental City." These same visitors might have been invited to a ball at the Assembly Room, a theatrical production at the Holliday Street Theatre, or an exhibition at one of the numerous halls established for such ventures. In short, visitors would have been struck by the industry and possibilities offered by this city on the rise. Baltimore was a complex mixture of small-town charm and big-city sophistication.[4]

Despite its economic development, Baltimore's social organization remained Southern. Visitors traveling from North to South usually noted that Baltimore was the first place where they glimpsed Southern culture. They frequently commented on the hospitality and refinements that they observed. At the same time, most visitors to antebellum Baltimore indicated that they saw little poverty; there were no tenements. Even as late as 1858, when industrial growth meant a large population of laborers, the Board of Health's annual report noted that "there is, perhaps, no city in which the industrial and laboring classes are better housed."[5] There was no strict housing segregation, although most of the social, commercial, and professional leaders lived downtown on Gay Street, regarded as the fashionable center of town. Poorer citizens tended to live on the outskirts of town, while those with medium wealth usually were spread throughout the city—typical of most Southern cities during this period. Many poor whites and free blacks lived in the Spring Garden section, an industrial section packed with "mechanics, labourers, and coloured population."[6]

Nearly 50 percent of the slaves lived downtown—which was also typical. Slaveholding in Baltimore did differ from Norfolk and Richmond in one respect, however. Only a small portion of white families owned slaves—the lowest incidence of slaveholding in any border city during the antebellum period.[7] Another difference from Norfolk and Richmond was the frequency of street disturbances, so much so that Baltimore picked up the nickname "Mobtown" early in the nineteenth century. Most of the disturbances were responses to bank failures or political quarrels; many involved street gangs of white youths. Historians have found it difficult to explain the disturbances. The city's transient waterfront population, the rapid growth, and the number of street gangs have all been offered as explanations.[8]

Located on a peninsula bordered on one side by the Elizabeth River and the other by the Chesapeake Bay, and with the advantage of a deep harbor, Norfolk was convenient to the Atlantic Ocean. Consequently, although it was much smaller than Baltimore, Norfolk was still a commercial center and port in its own right, serving Virginia's lower tidewater. Visitors took notice of the shipbuilding works and the large warehouses, particularly tobacco warehouses, near the docks. In contrast to Baltimore and Richmond, Norfolk's commerce was not complemented by industrial development. Norfolk also offered fewer leisure choices, a result, it seems, of its small population rather than of attitudes toward amusement. Nevertheless, even at the opening of the century inquiring visitors would have found plenty to keep them amused, ranging from the theater and museum to various taverns and pleasure gardens. As the century progressed, additional amusement choices, including such things as exhibitions, circuses, and lectures, provided entertainment to responsive audiences.

Norfolk had a reputation for being orderly. Visitors noted that the citizens were genteel and agreeable, but not as cosmopolitan as the inhabitants of Baltimore or Richmond. Tourists visiting Norfolk during the last decade of the eighteenth century and the first decades of the nineteenth century were also fairly unanimous in their assessment of Norfolk's development: it was a town that had seen better days but was attempting a comeback.[9] During the first three decades of the century, Norfolk was nearly destroyed several times by "destructive conflagrations"—fires that swept viciously through the wooden houses and buildings. By 1828 many of the wooden structures had been replaced with brick buildings. Even the sometimes cranky visitor Anne Royall observed that while she had "expected to have seen an old, dirty-looking, gloomy, clownish town," she saw, "on the contrary" that "the houses are large and elegant, and many of them surrounded with beautiful trees. . . . The town is not only neat, it is beautiful." She noted the "well paved" and "lighted" streets, which she thought were the "neatest kept in any town in the Union, except Providence."[10]

Beyond the older part of the city, which fronted the water, the area encompassed by Freemason and Granby streets was the fashionable part of town; tourists commented upon the beautiful houses and flower gardens. Many noticed the contrast between the numerous church spires and the flatness of the landscape. The one blight on the town was the marshy area around Back Creek, between the old town and Freemason

Street. Despite attempts to fill in the area, the problem, and its associated stench, remained until after the Civil War.[11]

13

Situated at the fall line of the James River, Richmond served the upper tidewater and the piedmont of Virginia. Visitors arriving in Richmond noticed the stark contrast between the low land around the river and the steep hills rising nearby to the north. Travel literature of the nineteenth century is replete with descriptions of both the beautiful houses on the hills and the dirty, unpaved streets of the downtown area. Mrs. Basil Hall noted in 1827 that "Richmond is beautifully situated, but it is a vilely dirty place."[12] In 1844 George Featherstonhaugh contrasted the upper town with its "cheerful villa-looking houses" with "the lower town, which swarms with negro coal-heavers, . . . one of the dirtiest places in America."[13]

Approaching the city from the river, visitors to Richmond in the first decades of the century would have first noticed the masts of large ships and the bustle of activity along the wharves. Tourists new to Richmond might have been surprised by the amount of industrial development located on the river's northern bank. Heading west on Main Street, which ran parallel to the river, these same visitors would have passed the open market and crossed Shockoe Creek, where boys liked to swim and fish while their mothers and sisters did laundry. Continuing up Main Street on Shockoe Hill, the visitors would have passed taverns and stores, as well as several coffeehouses. Farther north, in the area bounded by Broad Street, they would have passed several theaters and exhibition halls, as well as a museum and more taverns. They might have stopped to take in the beauty of the state Capitol, noting how majestic Thomas Jefferson's design seemed on the hill above the river.

The neighborhoods in Richmond tended to follow the topography. The fashionable neighborhood was located on the hills just north of the Capitol. Here wealthy whites and their slaves lived together and separately. Free blacks and middle-class whites occupied dwellings on the streets that sloped down to the river. Poorer folk tended to congregate in neighborhoods in the low areas and on the edge of the city. East of Shockoe Hill, on the north end of Church Hill, Shad Town had developed near the site of a brickyard. Butchertown, in the valley between Shockoe and Church hills, was a rough place with slaughterhouses, tanneries, soap factories, and a foul odor attributed to a stagnant pond containing the runoff from the local industries. Likewise, the area near

Baltimore, Norfolk, and Richmond

the river—Rocketts, the Basin, and Penitentiary Bottom—was home to a motley crowd of day laborers, hired-out slaves from the tobacco factories, runaways, seamen, slave merchants, and trading agents. West of town was a section known as Screamersville, where there were grog-shops and cheap boardinghouses patronized primarily by poor whites and blacks.[14]

Richmond was the leading commercial and industrial center of Virginia; by 1860 it ranked thirteenth of all cities in the United States in the value of its manufactures. Richmond was known for its flour mills, including the Gallego mill, the largest in the world. In 1860 more than four hundred thousand barrels of flour, valued at more than three million dollars, were milled in Richmond, most of it being shipped to South America in exchange for coffee. The output of the Richmond flour mills was almost equal to that of the four to five dozen mills in the Baltimore area, the Atlantic Coast's other great milling center.[15] Tobacco factories and ironworks were the other major manufacturing concerns in Richmond. In 1819 the city directory listed eleven tobacco factories; by 1860 there were fifty factories. Slaves made up a large part of the antebellum work force. They were a majority of the workers in the tobacco industry and worked in the metal shops, particularly the Tredegar Iron Works, as well as the large flour mills.[16]

Leisure in all three cities was influenced by their locations. Summer was particularly unbearable in these low-lying regions; the oppressive heat and humidity combined to halt much activity. The real scourge of these cities in the summer, however, was the outbreak of epidemic diseases, particularly cholera and yellow fever. Yellow fever struck Baltimore in 1800, 1819, and 1820; while Norfolk was visited in 1821 and 1826 and nearly devastated by a three-month epidemic in 1855. Those who were able to leave usually fled to the country to visit friends or traveled to the Virginia mountains. The rest remained on constant alert for rumors of disease.[17] Epidemics spread, also, as people fled from one city to another and carried disease with them.[18] Municipal authorities attempted to prevent public gatherings in close places during the summer. Early theatrical licensing laws in Baltimore, for example, prohibited productions from June 10 to October 1. The ordinance of 1797 noted that "the Collecting of great numbers of people during the Warm Season, into Theatres, is productive of Contagious diseases and other

Maladies." [19] Given the dangers and the concern, it is significant that in the nineteenth century public amusements and favorable response to them increased, even in the summer. It is also important to underscore that the numerous epidemic outbreaks, as well as the disruptions caused by the Civil War, did not alter this trend.

.. 15 ..

The attitudes toward amusement and amusement patronage in the three cities disclosed the prevailing social values there. Amusements provided important outlets for social intercourse; consequently, issues of democracy, social status, cultural control, class division, and respectability were inextricably intertwined with the ongoing arguments about the propriety of amusement. Society in Baltimore, Norfolk, and Richmond was, paradoxically, both open and highly structured. Movement between social classes, particularly from lower to middle, was fairly easy. At the same time, despite the egalitarian rumblings of Jacksonian democracy, social stratification was a fact of life. In 1824 John H. B. Latrobe noted that social division was increasing as the cities grew. The absence of hereditary rank encouraged citizens to create their own divisions. [20] Mary Boykin Chesnut could not get over the emphasis on social status in Richmond; she was particularly appalled by the use of the term "F.F.V." to describe those who were descendants of the first families of Virginia. Although social distinctions lessened during the Civil War period, they quickly reappeared once the war was over. Those recognized as the "First Families" were quite aware of their position and, consequently, their duties, including leadership in social affairs. [21]

The upper class in Baltimore, Norfolk, and Richmond was composed of physicians, politicians, the most eminent lawyers, wealthy planters, and powerful merchants. Writing in 1851, John P. Little described Richmond's upper class, noting its leadership in the realm of leisure:

The higher circle consisted of the families of the neighboring planters, who left their estates to the management of overseers, and spent the larger part of the year in Richmond, because of its social advantages. To these were added the better class of merchants and resident citizens, and the State officers with their families. . . . They were men of leisure who spent life in enjoyment; they were not money makers, nor did they feel the cares and anxieties of men of trade; their leisure and their natural disposition led them to cultivate those occupations and amusements which rather refine the manners and add to our happiness, than those which increase the wealth and prosperity of a community.[22]

During the early years of the century this group was descended from the older settlers and was tightly knit by propinquity and intermarriage. In Baltimore and Richmond, industrialists and entrepreneurs gradually replaced the old gentry. Norfolk's elite, however, was not as broad-based, remaining predominantly commercial.[23]

Citizens of Richmond had a curious term that they applied to the upper social stratum—"upper tendom" or "upper tendum." A visitor to Richmond in 1854, Miss Mendell, was amused when one of the residents told her that "it was now the height of the ambition of the citizens to get a 'place' on Shokkoe Hill, which, I suppose for this, is *the* hill, and belongs exclusively to 'upper-tendom.'"[24] During the ravages of the Civil War a Richmonder wrote: "While battle and famine encompass us on every hand upper-tendom is as gay as though peace and plenty blessed the land."[25] In 1867 John Langbourne Williams attended a wedding at St. James's Church in Richmond and noted that "all upper tendum was represented."[26]

Although collectively the upper class in all three cities was very powerful and influential in the nineteenth century, especially in the antebellum period, the actions and writings of the upper-class citizens suggest that some were genuinely concerned lest they lose their status and slip from their positions of authority. This anxiety about status seems less paradoxical when the dynamic nature of social relations is noted. Classes were present, but the system was not closed. While the upper-class gentry did, as a group, continue to influence the economic, political, and social life of these cities, membership in the upper class was not static.

Some members of the old upper class found their status challenged by newcomers—often newly wealthy entrepreneurs and industrialists—and they responded with various attempts to distinguish themselves from those with less status and maintain their ranks. This sentiment is vividly illustrated in a letter that David Campbell wrote to fellow Virginian Claiborne W. Gooch in July 1818 regarding representation in the General Assembly. Noting that it was relatively easy for men to acquire wealth and move into positions of power, Campbell urged Gooch to join him in preventing such takeovers: "We, who have once taken our stand at the head of columns, must keep our rank everywhere."[27]

The small but growing middle class was composed of shopkeepers, small merchants, lesser lawyers, educators, and ministers. Although they were not social leaders in the way the upper-class citizens were, some middle-class citizens—particularly ministers, journalists, and educators—were outspoken critics or advocates of particular amusements. In a sense, they set the moral tone for society; they were the cultural leaders. As the century progressed and the upper class further removed itself from ordinary society, the middle class played a major role in defining proper behavior. In this way middle-class citizens distinguished themselves from the rougher elements of the lower class, while also occasionally assuming moral superiority to the upper class.

The large lower class consisted of mechanics and artisans, common laborers, free blacks, and farm workers—primarily people who worked in some way for others, particularly for upper- or upper-middle-class bosses. Although Baltimore, Norfolk, and Richmond were not as industrialized as cities of the North, workers were beginning to become aware of themselves as a status group, if not a class, particularly in Baltimore and Richmond. At the same time, there was no well-developed working-class culture comparable to what existed in cities such as Boston, Worcester, Pittsburgh, or Cincinnati by mid-century. In part, this might be attributed to the number of slaves and/or free blacks in the labor force. While Irish and German laborers began to displace free blacks from some unskilled jobs in Baltimore in the 1850s, blacks maintained jobs as oystermen, seamen, and bricklayers. Likewise, both slaves and free blacks remained a strong part of the work force in Richmond, especially in the tobacco factories. In Richmond in 1860 there were 174 skilled free blacks: 33 barbers, 27 plasterers, 27 carpenters, 22 blacksmiths, 17 shoemakers, and 16 bricklayers.[28]

At the beginning of the century, the lower class could often be found in amusement crowds with the middle and upper classes. By the middle of the century, some lower-class citizens were enjoying their own amusements; sometimes these met with middle-class approval, sometimes they did not. Also by mid-century, the lower class consisted of two disparate groups: those who were conscious of the value of self-improvement and those who were hopelessly stuck at the bottom. The former group's awareness of the relationship of self-improvement to upward mobility was often reflected in its amusement choices.

At the bottom of the social scale were the slaves. Because of their unique position, they could often be found with upper-class citizens at amusements simply because they were forced to accompany them there. House servants sometimes imitated the amusements and social pretensions of whites. In 1860 Samuel Mordecai noted that the slave "gentry" of Richmond enjoyed dressing up and promenading on Sunday, leaving visiting cards in much the same way as their masters. Generally, however, slaves had their own amusements, which were informal, unstructured, and without significant cost. Slaves in Richmond had a great amount of autonomy; they were often allowed to hire themselves out and find their own lodgings. In the tobacco factories, they could even earn bonuses for production above quota. This independence extended to social life, which was often centered on the church. There was also a tradition of benevolence thorough work in clandestine societies. Slave social life in Norfolk was limited by the imposition of curfews: nine P.M. in summer and eight P.M. in winter.[29]

Churches in the three cities were divided fairly strictly along social lines. In 1833 Scottish visitor Stephen Davis noted that Richmond's Baptist churches had a large "portion of coloured people"—at least 1,400 black members in one congregation.[30] In 1835 Andrew Reed reported that both the Baptist and Methodist congregations of Richmond were predominantly black.[31] In contrast, St. Paul's Episcopal Church was, as one visitor noted in 1854, "the fashionable Congregation."[32] In 1839 a visitor to Baltimore recorded that "the Unitarian Church, near the Cathedral" and St. Paul's Episcopal Church were "frequented by the fashionable," while in 1841 another visitor to Baltimore observed that "in the Methodist Church the poor and humble formed the majority of the worshippers." Cemeteries in the three cities reflected a similar social hierarchy.[33]

Social stratification was also evident in amusements. Over the course of the century social divisions within particular amusements increased—more seating gradations, for example. Gradually there was also more stratification of amusements themselves, the patterns of stratification changing during the nineteenth century. Social status, age, sex, income, occupation, residence, education, and interests all helped to determine

amusement choices and shape amusement forms.[34] By mid-century
amusements were divided along fairly strict class lines; social status
played a major role in the determination of leisure choices. Nevertheless,
it should be noted that the stratification of amusements mirrored the
shifting relations between classes. The class system was dynamic, not
static; as class memberships shifted and changed and notions of class
changed, the stratification of amusements also shifted and changed.

By mid-century, amusement choice was itself beginning to serve as a
vehicle of social status. This grew to be very important during the
antebellum period as new wealth began to displace some of the older
families. Even young children perceived the relationship between wealth
and status and wrote about the necessity of money for proper living.[35]
Ancestry was not enough; money was the key, as a young Baltimore
woman underscored in describing the decline of a Baltimore belle: "You
know what a belle Pully was last winter, every body admired both her
appearance and manner, this winter when she was in town she was
scarcely attended to—The difference between the rich Miss Howard
daughter of the governor and the same person without fortune or
title!!!"[36]

Amusement choices often served as a means of expressing and maintaining status in the face of such changes. Early in the century this did
not always entail separate amusements. Upper-class citizens accommo-
dated themselves to the existing framework, seeking segregation by
virtue of seating arrangements, special social groups and clubs, and
exclusive parties. As the century progressed, however, there was a
noticeable change. The upper class sought to develop its own amusements, often giving up or modifying those that had been taken up by
people with lower status. Meanwhile, middle-class citizens also saw that
amusement choices could confer social status, and they responded in
several ways. Often they adopted upper-class amusements; in addition,
they came up with their own definition of gentility, which included what
they believed to be proper amusement participation. This definition also
influenced the amusement choices of that segment of the lower class that
aspired to self-improvement.

More important, the use of amusement to express or achieve status led
to greater participation in amusements, particularly amusements that
were pure entertainment and had no redeeming educational value. Donald J. Mrozek's study of the rise of respectability of sport indicates that

Baltimore, Norfolk, and Richmond

the acceptance of sport hinged on the frequency of its occurrence; "once sport achieved a certain frequency and distribution, it tended to generate new conditions and advance its own acceptance."[37] Similarly, it appears that the frequent participation of all classes in public amusements led to the gradual acceptance of popular commercial amusements as a given part of everyday life.

Chapter Two

The Exhibition, Museum, and Lecture: Education or Entertainment?

.. One afternoon in 1818 a large, rather exuberant crowd was gathered on one of Baltimore's hills. All sorts of people were there—some poor, some prominent. One of those in the crowd was a visitor, John Duncan, who later recorded his impressions in a letter. Duncan noted that "plenty of all classes" were present, including "females of various ages, and apparently all conditions." Becoming acquainted with two women who were standing near him, Duncan had offered them the use of his perspective glass. He observed that they "continued to use it alternately till the whole melancholy scene was over." [1] Similar scenes were repeated many times in Baltimore, Norfolk, and Richmond during the nineteenth century. The occasion was not a parade or circus, or even a fair; rather, the attraction was a public execution.

Known by some as a "Carnival of Death," the public execution was a source of free—if macabre—entertainment. Descriptions from all three cities indicate that thousands of people gathered on such occasions. One of the most popular Richmond carnivals occurred on August 27, 1827, when three Spanish pirates were executed for murder. Approximately 7,000 spectators gathered in the natural amphitheater created by the hills northeast of the penitentiary to watch the gruesome show. Jacob Frey reminisced that at least 30,000 people turned out to witness the execution of a man named Adam Horn in Baltimore in 1844. Sometimes curiosity was joined with sympathy. At least 5,000 people gathered in Norfolk on October 23, 1863, to view the hanging of a much loved local physician, David M. Wright. Wright had been sentenced to death for killing another white man, a Union captain who was in command of a company of black soldiers. The crowd showed great respect for the condemned man, whom they considered a martyr to the Southern cause.[2]

Generally the proceedings followed a set form. First there was a parade—really, a mock parade—featuring the convicted criminal (or criminals) on the way to the gallows. Sometimes the convict was forced to walk, but often he or she was displayed on a cart or in a cage on a cart. The Spanish pirates walked down Main Street wearing purple robes and hoods, with hanging ropes around their necks.[3] After some preliminary comments from a local authority, the convicted criminal usually made a few remarks. Following that, a local clergyman addressed the crowd, often at length, about the consequences of evil. Then, the crowd waited quietly for the fatal moment. Depending on the circumstances, sometimes the crowd responded with hushed murmurs, while at other times the spectators erupted into cheering.

The public execution was not merely a time for festivity; it also verified the effectiveness of the legal system. Citizens could see what happened to those who broke the law. Children were admonished to be good or face similar tragic ends. Admittedly the Carnival of Death is a curious example of nineteenth-century amusement. It does, however, suggest the mixture of education and entertainment in many amusements—especially exhibitions, museums, and lectures—during this period. Examination of these amusements, which generally had a middle-class following, offers the opportunity to see how the tension between education and entertainment found expression in the nineteenth century. The emphasis on education prevailed during the early years of the century. As the century progressed, there were two major lines of development. First, the definition of education broadened to include things that were entertainment—popular science, for example. In addition, the public became increasingly receptive to programs that were pure entertainment.

During the first part of the century, an educational program was usually morally uplifting. Exhibitions of ancient history or biblical themes drew praise for their beauty, but they were valued primarily for the lessons they inspired. A communication in the *Baltimore American* in June 1817 discussed the value of an exhibition of Italian art that depicted scenes from ancient history. The author commended the artistry but emphasized the moral, suggesting that the study of ancient themes had become "a necessary part of the education of the youth of both sexes."[4]

Similarly, wax exhibits, paintings, and panoramas usually represented biblical or historical figures or events, a point that advertisements stressed. Exhibition promoters urged fathers to bring their families to view inspirational people or events. Children were admitted for half price; special matinee showings were open for children and women. A panorama of the Battle of North Point, featuring 230 square feet of canvas, drew large crowds in Baltimore in 1815. The Battle of Waterloo and the Battle of Moscow were also popular subjects.[5] Crowds marveled at models and paintings of Jerusalem and depictions of Christ's life. In Baltimore in 1829 a painting of the destruction of Sodom was billed as "family viewing." When inclement weather prevented a number of people from viewing this work, several men of the community who wanted "to have an opportunity of bring their families" convinced the proprietor to leave it in Baltimore for ten more days, or so his advertisement said.[6]

Even when subjects were more contemporary, they usually taught a lesson. In Baltimore in October 1815, Mr. Mallet's Academy was advertising the addition of a wax figure resembling a "FEMALE NEGRO well known to the public in the streets of this city, and remarkable for her respectful salutations of those she meets."[7] No doubt the person depicted was a slave frequently seen in the city market, one whose positive outlook on life supported the existing social system and later helped to justify the "peculiar institution." Little children could learn more from an afternoon viewing such figures than a dozen lectures on their society's values could teach them.

Panoramas of important towns of the United States showed the value of industry—of the work ethic. Often these exhibitions featured mechanical parts, which depicted work. In 1825, for example, a panorama in Baltimore showed a "Commercial and Manufacturing City, with the inhabitants at their various employments, the whole set in motion by machinery." These exhibits often approached life size; an advertisement for a panorama in Baltimore in 1813 indicated that the display was 30 feet by 18 feet by 15 feet.[8]

The most morally uplifting exhibits were those that glorified the natural world and underscored the benevolence of God. The interest in animals and plants reflected the growing interest in the natural sciences,

The Exhibition, Museum, and Lecture

as opposed to the physical sciences. Proprietors of these shows appealed to their patrons' curiosity about natural life. Peale's Museum in Baltimore, for example, was established in 1813 to exhibit a mastodon skeleton that Charles Willson Peale had unearthed in rural New York. Peale's son Rembrandt Peale first toured England with the skeleton before returning to the states with it.[9] During the early years of the century, the residents of Baltimore, Norfolk, and Richmond turned out to view live Bengal tigers, American elks, African leopards, African lions, Arabian camels, llamas, orangutans, African apes, long-tailed marmosets, dancing pigs, dancing turkeys, elephants, anteaters, rattlesnakes, and copperheads. In 1823 a major drawing card at Peale's Museum was the "Gruesome Exhibition" of the head of a New Zealand chief. Advertisements invited prospective audiences to view the head "of a chief who was conquered and embalmed . . . and preserved by the victorious party." In 1827 a large Baltimore crowd paid to see a section of a large tree that measured 18 feet in circumference. Peale's also exhibited popular touring oddities such as P. T. Barnum's "Fejee Mermaid."[10]

In line with the interest in the natural world and the bounty of nature, crowds acclaimed exhibitions of performers who had unusual physical or mental talents. Crowds admired ventriloquists, mimics, and magicians because of their "astonishing powers" of voice or movement. They also praised statuary displays, presentations featuring gymnasts who mimicked statues. In 1802 Norfolk crowds marveled at a pair of gymnasts who imitated birds, completed back somersaults from three tables and a chair, leaped over twelve men with fixed bayonets, and finished with the "Antipodean Whirligig" in which one performer "whirled on his head at the rate of 250 a minute, without the assistance of his hands."[11]

American crowds responded to the simplest human feats with expressions of awe and amazement, as British traveler Henry Fearon noted in 1818 when visiting Washington: "In this city I also witnessed the exhibitions of SEMA SAMA, the Indian juggler, from London. My chief attention was directed to the audience; their disbelief of the possibility of performing the numerous feats advertised, and their inconceivable surprise at witnessing the actual achievement, appeared extreme— approaching almost a childish wonder and astonishment."[12]

Audiences were similarly awestruck by the various mechanical and scientific exhibitions that were popular during the early years of the century. Proprietors realized that people were interested in how things worked—the scientific laws that served as a basis for the working of the natural world—and therefore made outrageous claims about their machines. One visitor to Richmond in 1829 poked fun at some of the capabilities attributed to a microscope then on exhibit: "Tomorrow I design to visit the *Solar Microscope,* now exhibiting in the city, where I shall see *eels six feet long* spoiling in a drop of common vinegar, Varments as large *as common shoats* making battle in a Fig. *Alligators Crocidiles* and a host of *Snapping Turtles* contending for the mastery in our most common articles of diet. Verily I fear I shall not enjoy an appetite for ten days to come."[13]

Proprietors, in fact, could get away with a lot as long as they made a pretense of moralizing. The public enjoyed animated biblical exhibitions in which "most of the principal figures open and shut their eyes in an astonishing manner, highly resembling natural life."[14] Exhibition promoters also were careful to assure the public that their nonbiblical programs were morally sound. The proprietor of an exhibition of Androides, animated automatons, informed Norfolk audiences in 1827 that the subject was not sacrilegious.[15] The promoter of an exhibition of fireworks in Baltimore in 1829 indicated that there should be no objections to his show for it was innocent in content. He called for the patronage and approbation of all classes of the community."[16]

Like the proprietors of exhibitions, operators of museums stressed that their institutions provided positive education or "innocent recreation." Again, biblical or historical themes predominated. The Richmond Museum, which opened in October 1817, was less successful than its Baltimore counterpart, primarily because of the competition from other exhibitions. Nevertheless, it served one segment of the population well. Nineteenth-century historian Samuel Mordecai noted that "children constituted the far greater number" of its visitors.[17] The museums of Baltimore also strived to attract "ladies of the first respectability" and children. Advertisements stressed the moral value of visiting a museum, and "friends of innocent amusement" were thanked for their patronage.[18] In the 1830s one visitor to Baltimore who was not impressed with the sophistication of a museum exhibit noted that the major item was advertised as "a splendid moral picture of Adam and Eve" and observed that it attracted primarily children.[19]

During the 1840s and 1850s the content of most exhibitions changed and the definition of educational broadened. Moral themes gave way to

The Exhibition, Museum, and Lecture

more secular ones, while popular science, especially flamboyant experiments, replaced natural science. The exhibition began to serve as a showcase for curiosities and freaks—as an entertainment center. Exhibitions ranged from the ridiculous to the perverse. One of the sillier exhibits was the "industrial fleas" program presented in Baltimore in 1830. One woman who had seen this exhibition recalled that the owner "had spent twenty years of his life learning to harness two fleas, or four, to tiny buggies or carriages *perfectly* made, of tissue paper, and also to dress his fleas in garments of the same." She noted that all of her friends went to see "this ridiculous curiosity."[20]

Exhibition promoters took people from exotic countries and turned them into curiosities or celebrities. One Chinese woman, Afong Moy, made several tours of Southern cities as a display piece. Besides her nationality, Afong Moy's other drawing card was her tiny feet, a fact that did not go unnoticed in the press. A Baltimore writer noted that her shoes were the size of a one-year-old infant's because she had "worn iron shoes for the first ten years of her life, according to the custom of the country."[21] The Richmond advertisements underscored that Afong Moy was part of the first Chinese display in America, but the focus was on her feet. One bill noted that she would "occasionally walk before the Company on an elevated stage in order that her *extraordinary little feet* may be seen to advantage."[22] One young girl returned from the exhibition in Baltimore and indicated that she was more favorably impressed than she thought she would be, especially since she "had heard so much of her feet being disgusting."[23]

The really disgusting exhibits, however, were those animals and human freaks that were advertised as "LIVING CURIOSITIES." Such was the double cow that had "3 hips, 2 tails, 5 perfect legs, and 6 feet," billed, naturally, as "THE ONLY ONE IN THE WORLD."[24] Ostensibly the cow was of interest to the natural scientists, but it is more likely that the interest was of a baser nature. An advertisement for Lewis the Virginia dwarf suggested the dual nature of such exhibitions: "To the Naturalist the dwarf Lewis presents himself as a remarkable subject for Philosophic observation—to the curious he furnishes readily an object of singularly rare attention."[25]

Popular midgets such as General Tom Thumb, Commodore Foote, Colonel Small, the Fairy of the West, Commodore Nutt, and Miss

Minnie Warren, as well as the various bearded ladies, giants, and giantesses, attracted throngs of curious gawkers because they were oddities. Certainly the Siamese twins Chang and Eng Bunker were anatomical specimens; but most people who came to gaze at them were more interested in their private lives, especially how they managed to father twenty-two children. Some could view Tom Thumb as the sort of oddity that showed Nature's bounty, as Neil Haris suggests; but many were more interested in him because he was a freak.[26]

The language of much of the advertising also indicates the true nature of these exhibits. Sounding like a come-on from a circus barker, the bill for fourteen-year-old Mitchell Jarco emphasized the unfortunate boy's deformities: "He has no knees, nor joints, from the hips to the ankles: has two sets, or double rows, of front teeth, &c." displaying in his person the wildest freak of nature perhaps in the known world."[27] An exhibition of natural wonders at the Baltimore Museum of Anatomy was billed as "Thrilling and Startling Wonders, Curiosities and Freaks of Nature."[28] In 1868 the Siamese twins did not even receive nominal billing as natural specimens. Rather, they were automatically lumped with other "curiosities."[29]

Magicians and wizards, as well as chemical and optical experiments, appeared to be more a sideshow than science. Programs were often billed as "scientific entertainment"; seances and clairvoyant exhibitions, for example, were both scientific and entertaining. There were some biblical references—one magician promised to "call spirits from air, and Fairies from the vastly deep . . . change a rod into a Serpent, and water into wine"—but the emphasis was no longer religious.[30]

Museum proprietors had learned early in the century that they could exhibit almost anything if they labeled it as educational. They continued to stretch the definition to include the unusual and bizarre—things that would attract curious patrons. Baltimore theater historian Alonzo May noted that Peale's Museum was "patronized by Ministers and others who were conscientiously opposed to Theatres, yet saw no objection to visiting an establishment confessedly devoted to the preservation of freaks of all descriptions."[31] Peale, who skillfully drummed up support by occasionally donating an evening's proceeds to the poor, often introduced things that were supposedly of special interest to his Baltimore audience. British visitor Joseph Pickering noted that Peale had proudly told him "how he had duped the natives by an introduction of a tune into his organ, called the Berkshire fencibles, as a new tune, by the name of the Baltimore volunteers, which gave him a great run."[32]

The lecture similarly evolved from an educational to an entertaining medium. Early nineteenth-century lectures usually had featured a serious speaker discussing historical, political, or religious topics. By the 1840s and 1850s the popular lecturer was more than likely an accomplished showman who often involved members of the audience in his act. Yet, because the program was, supposedly, a lecture of sorts, those who thought it sinful to use leisure solely for enjoyment could attend with eased consciences. The term "illustrated lecture," with its positive connotations, sometimes was used as a euphemism for productions of questionable content. Thus, in 1847 Dr. Hollick lectured in Richmond on the "PHILOSOPHY AND PHYSIOLOGY OF THE ORIGIN OF LIFE." Women and youths were barred from the show, which was illustrated with "SIXTEEN SPLENDID, FULL SIZED, LIFE-LIKE MODELS, representing the whole human organization complete in *both systems and at every stage of development*"—a move calculated to attract a crowd.[33] An Italian lecturing in Richmond in 1842 called volunteers from the crowd as subjects, displaying his ability to deduce character from their facial features. One woman who attended this lecture was struck by the Italian's "astonishing powers" of discerning the characters of the audience "as if he had known us all our lives."[34] A professor stirred considerable excitement in Norfolk in 1845 with a series of lectures on animal magnetism. He accompanied his talks with bizarre experiments that attracted great crowds.[35]

Beginning in the late 1840s celebrities were also an important drawing card on the lecture circuit. Again, there was educational justification—the speakers were usually prominent authors, scientists, or ministers—but it is hard to escape the conclusion that often the crowds were more interested in seeing the person than in hearing the talk. For example, Edgar Allan Poe lectured in Norfolk and Richmond in 1849 on "The Poetic Principle" and concluded by reading "The Raven." Poe's fame plus his Virginia connections were, no doubt, just as significant as his topic.[36] William Makepeace Thackeray gave a series of lectures in Baltimore and Richmond in 1853 that drew large audiences. His topics were "Swift," "Congreve and Addison," and "Steele and the Times of Queen Anne." An account of one of the lectures by a woman in the audience, however, did not even mention the topic. Rather, she indicated her awe of Thackeray and noted that she was glad that he liked the audience.[37] Thackeray himself expressed surprise at seeing a crowd "of little school girls" at another of his Richmond lectures in 1856. Apparently the topic dealt with the "favorites of the four Georges," not exactly a subject intended for children.[38]

The evolution of the lecture did not go unnoticed by critics. Writing in *Scribner's Monthly* in February 1872, J. G. Holland castigated the change in the lecture: "There was a time, when a lecture was a lecture. The men who appeared before the lyceums were men who had something to say. . . . Now, a lecture may be any string of nonsense that any literary montebank can find an opportunity to utter. Artemus Ward 'lectured': and he was right royally paid for acting the literary buffoon. He has had many imitators, and the damage that he and they have inflicted upon the institution of the lyceum is incalculable."[39]

The change in the lecture topics presented by the mechanics' institutes in the three cities vividly illustrates the evolution of the lecture. The institutes offered annual series of public lectures that were aimed particularly at young men in mechanical occupations. In 1835 an editor of the *Norfolk and Portsmouth Herald* praised the Norfolk Mechanics Institute for providing instruction in the use of leisure: "The Institution if rightly managed will be of incalculable benefit, not only in disseminating useful knowledge generally, but in the improvement of the minds and morals of our youth who are engaged in mechanical occupations, by presenting to them a rational and instructive mode of employing their leisure hours, the abuse of which in idle and debasing amusements, has so often made shipwreck of the character and prospects of that class of our young men."[40] The Maryland Institute for Promotion of the Mechanic Arts began in 1829 by offering practical instruction to workingmen and their families. The 1851–52 course opened with a lecture by the Honorable J. R. Chandler on "The Position, Duties, and Responsibilities of the Mechanic." One commentator noted that the result in Baltimore, and elsewhere, was "the elevation of mechanical arts . . . by force of their example and teaching."[41]

By the late 1850s, however, the emphasis on the practical education of mechanics had been superseded by an accent on topics that were more general, and often more entertaining. In part, of course, this was related to the changing composition of the audience. The institutes were attempting to attract more people who were not mechanics, particularly women. The Maryland Institute's 1857–58 course opened with a fairly abstract and philosophical lecture entitled "Slowness as a Law of Progress."[42] The 1859 season at the Mechanics Institute in Richmond was a little more lively. In January a crowd turned out to hear Mr. Stephen Massett, a "vocalist, composer, mimic, and elocutionist." In March a writer in the *Richmond Enquirer* wittily commented on the allures of a performer at the same hall "who kicked up and showed off her little *jokes jambes*" and led "the city *bon ton* into dangerous ecstasy."[43] In 1865 Dr. B. Brown Williams was packing the Maryland Institute with "his curious and marvelous experiment of making men DRUNK ON COLD WATER, Together with *five hundred* other astonishing and amusing mysteries of modern times."[44]

The growing significance of the entertainment aspect of amusements is similarly observed in relatives of the museum and exhibition. The American circus, for example, had characteristics of both. It originally had served as a source of fellowship and education. Families went to see exotic animals, horsemanship, and gymnastic performances. As the century progressed, however, the circus's emphasis changed from diversion and instruction to dazzlement. Managers of freak exhibits and pseudoscientific machinations took advantage of the public's tendency to focus on nature and scientific laws. Language couched in semitechnological or semibiological terms attracted attention, but the exhibits, especially when organized in grand circus style, bedazzled the audiences.[45]

Another relative of the exhibition, the agricultural fair, underwent a comparable evolution. Originally horticultural or agricultural shows that featured cattle and displays of crops and machinery, the fairs drew country folk to town to participate or view. Sponsored by agricultural and horticultural societies, the fairs were instructional in nature.[46] By the mid-fifties, however, the fairs had changed. Competition became an important reason for both exhibitors and spectators to attend. President Millard Fillmore, for example, visited the Baltimore Agricultural Fair in 1853 to view a plowing match. Fairs began to feature balloon ascensions, military and fire company parades, and jousting tournaments. There was something for everyone, even those with no interest in agriculture. Women were encouraged to visit "to give animation and beauty to the occasion." The Richmond fair of 1857 coincided with a visit of "Wyman the Wizard, with his egg-bag, 'Talking Tommie,' and other things that entertained tens of thousands of wondering men, women, and children."[47]

Parallels may be made in other areas as well. Because of connections with European artists, and thus European culture, musical entertainments were endowed with respectability and offered no challenge to the moral code. Astute promoters like P. T. Barnum took advantage of this sanction, however, by catering to the public taste and offering popular artists. Barnum's Jenny Lind was an artist who bridged the gap between culture and pure entertainment. She presented the image of a pious and moral young woman. Knowledge that she had given a command performance for Queen Victoria, as well as her generosity to charities, enhanced her reputation.[48] Barnum took pains to secure and maintain Lind's positive image. One Baltimore resident noted that Barnum invited Baltimore children to her concerts—a gesture calculated to attract popular approval: "The 'Queen of Song' was managed by the 'King of Advertisers,' and it entered his wise head that a good way to win a golden opinion in Baltimore was to invite all the high school—or was it all the public school children?—to a free treat."[49] Barnum's promotional efforts were successful. One Baltimore man told a friend that she should go hear Jenny Lind "to listen to the Efforts of one so distinguished."[50]

Neil Harris suggests that the public responded to Lind because "the dangerous passions that art could arouse were absent, subdued by the singer's noble soul and perfect technique."[51] Barnum himself noted that Lind's actual talent was virtually unknown before her American tour, suggesting that people initially turned out to see rather than hear her. She appealed to all classes. In Lind's case entertainment was justified by her personal life. As people became more comfortable with pure entertainment, however, it became less necessary for other promoters to have to justify their artists to the extent that Barnum did.[52]

Fritz Redlich's analysis of leisure suggests that the secularization of leisure activities in the nineteenth century was a consequence of the gradual movement from control by the church to control by business. Redlich notes that growing urban populations led to greater demand for "passive leisure" or spectator entertainments, which encouraged the involvement of business to provide funds, services, and equipment. Thus, Redlich concludes that secularization led to the commercializa-

The Exhibition, Museum, and Lecture

tion of leisure.[53] For the most part, analysis of amusements in Baltimore, Norfolk, and Richmond reaffirms this pattern. During the early years of the century, the clergy were very influential, as the emphasis on religious and moral themes suggests. By the middle of the century, however, they were losing control, in part because a more secular worldview was evolving in the urban areas.

It would, however, be wrong to underestimate the continuing influence of community leaders in Baltimore, Norfolk, and Richmond, for they continued to express middle- and upper-class fears and desires. Women also exerted a powerful, if subtle, influence over the community's standards. It would also be inaccurate to say that secularization preceded commercialization in Baltimore, Norfolk, and Richmond, for many of the early educational amusements that featured moral themes were commercial ventures.

In fact, the evidence suggests that the amusement entrepreneur who wished to be a successful businessman had to gauge the public temper. Commercial amusements during the early part of the nineteenth century often were not secular; if the public wanted moral themes, that is what it got. P. T. Barnum stressed that the secret of his success was his ability to discover and understand what his patrons wanted. Thus, he boasted that he had "abolished all vulgarity and profanity from the stage" and that "parents and children could attend" his shows and "not be shocked or offended by anything they might see or hear." As a result of his efforts, his shows often were reviewed in religious publications.[54] As the century progressed, promoters also became skilled at providing moral justification for new offerings. They often were aided by a press that tended to crown new attractions with overblown puffs. Thus, while secularization did not always precede commercialization, commercialization reinforced the movement toward the secular.

Astute promoters realized that patrons of organized popular amusements needed to feel comfortable with their amusement choices. Because the exhibition, museum, and lecture were amusements that originally were justified because they were educational, they offer a particularly vivid picture of the evolution toward inclusion of more "pure" entertainment in what were traditionally educational amusement forms in the nineteenth century. There was an obvious movement from a stress on education, in the moral and then in the scientific sense, to mixed education and entertainment, and finally to emphasis on entertainment itself. At the same time, the overlap should not be discounted, for it indicates the extent to which the acceptance of entertainment was ongoing in these amusements during the nineteenth century. There was always a mixture of education and entertainment, but in varying proportions.

Chapter Three

·•·

Public Behavior
and the Theater

·•· **O**n the evening of December 26, 1811, between 700 and 800 people were gathered in the Richmond Theatre for a program of plays. One of those present estimated that "every family in Richmond, or at least a very large portion of them" was represented. The removal of a chandelier during a stage change touched off a catastrophe; flames engulfed the scenery, and fire rapidly swept through the crowded hall. When the confusion had subsided, the death count was seventy-two, including twenty blacks. A list of the dead, described then as "some of Virginia's highest-toned characters, intellect, chivalry and accomplishments, mingled with plebian white and African," illustrates the mixed nature of theater crowds in early nineteenth-century Baltimore, Norfolk, and Richmond.[1]

The governor of Virginia, George W. Smith, and former United States senator and President of the Bank of Virginia Abraham B. Venable were among the fatalities. Benjamin Botts, who had served as Aaron Burr's defense attorney, made it to safety but returned to locate his wife in the blaze; both perished. Members of the state legislature were more fortunate. The *American Standard* marveled that although many of the legislators were present, not a single one lost his life.[2] Fifty of the disaster victims were women, and four of these were black. The disproportionate number of women was due in part to the highly flammable and cumbersome dresses that they wore, as well as their entrapment in the boxes. Some families who had come to the theater together lost several members before the night was over. Thomas Massie of Nelson County wrote his son, a doctor in Richmond, that when he heard about the fire he had feared that his son's entire family had been consumed in the disaster.[3]

Compared to the mostly middle-class patrons of educational amusements such as exhibitions or lectures, the early nineteenth-century theater crowds were much more diverse. Theater audiences included respectable men, women, and children; slaves and free blacks; and prostitutes and drunks. Unruly behavior was generalized throughout the audience, so much so that it was often difficult to determine the exact composition of the portion of the audience that provoked critics and earned the descriptive appellation "rowdies." The mixed nature of theater crowds had a lot to do with the form that the theater took in the nineteenth century. More than in any other nineteenth-century amusement, the audience played an active role in determining the content of programs, the shape of the amusement space, and the standards of crowd behavior.[4] Although drama critics berated the acting, clergy castigated the content, and those interested in safety worried about building construction, audiences enthusiastically turned out to see the latest offering. With the exception of the summer months, when municipal authorities sometimes prohibited the gathering of crowds inside theaters in order to prevent the transmission of diseases, theater in one form or another remained a popular amusement option for all social classes in the nineteenth century.[5]

Particularly during the first half of the century, theater parties often followed a grand dinner and served as the primary source of group entertainment for the upper class. Couples or groups usually purchased box seats and enjoyed visits with other boxholders as much as they enjoyed the performance. In Richmond, theater seasons that coincided with sessions of the legislature usually were very successful, because theater productions were a major form of evening entertainment. Thomas Green, a Richmond attorney who was a spectator at the Virginia Constitutional Convention of 1829–30, recorded that after enjoying dinner with a party that included former president James Madison and his wife Dolley, he joined most of the same group at the theater. It was quite an evening. In addition to Madison, the audience included former president James Monroe, as well as the Richmond Cavalry "in full uniform."[6]

It is not especially surprising that single men went to the theater by themselves or that men went together in a group. In the early antebellum years, women, particularly young single women, also attended theater productions with other women, without a male escort. Contemporaries did not consider this scandalous, and in fact, the practice was quite common until the 1840s. Typical of the respectable young women who often enjoyed an evening at the theater with friends, young Fanny Booth of Strawberry Hill near Richmond wrote a friend in 1820 detailing her plans to spend that evening with another friend at the Richmond Theatre. Apparently attending the show was more important than the substance of the show, for when she wrote, she still did not know what play was going to be performed.[7]

Although not so commonly, married women also occasionally went to the theater without a male escort. When Margaret Hunter Hall was visiting in Baltimore in 1827, she and her hostess took in a play while her husband, Basil, attended a bachelor party.[8] When a popular actor like Lucius Junius Booth was in town, women would line up and wait for hours to gain admission to the show. Theater managers often reserved a row or two of front seats for women, and these were especially coveted. Commenting on the crowd of women that filled the hall for a French Opera Review in Baltimore in 1829, a critic suggested that the event was more social than theatrical.[9]

Managers realized that winning the approbation of the women in a community went a long way toward insuring acceptance by the community at large. Young playgoers constituted another important segment of the theater audience; managers knew that theater habits formed at an early age would mean full houses in the future. Henry Tuckerman, who grew up in Baltimore in the second decade of the nineteenth century, reminisced that twice each season his parents allowed him to attend the Baltimore Theatre, which he considered one of his "great delights." Tuckerman and his friends spent hours discussing the "scenes, dialogues, jokes and startling messages about one thousand times" before filing the memories for recall later.[10]

Young people often staged their own amateur theatricals, putting on shows that emulated professional presentations. Theater manager John Hewitt wrote that *Faustus* and Theodore Edward Hook's *Tekeli* were both popular with Baltimore youth during the early part of the century when he was a boy. Hewitt described how, as he ventured around town early one evening, his "attention was drawn to a crowd of boys collected around the door of a decayed and dilapidated hovel, through whose walls a bright glare of light shone." He found a crowd of youths gathered to watch one of the amateur productions. One of the child actors was Nick

Robbins, who later attained fame at the Holliday Street Theatre in Baltimore.[11]

Blacks also were part of the typical theater audience. In the eighteenth century, slaves went to the theater early to secure places for their masters. As soon as the audience was seated, however, they usually were required to leave, a fact that advertisements often mentioned. During the early nineteenth century, in contrast, slaves often accompanied their masters to the theater and then stayed for the performance.[12] Occasionally, also, servants went to the theater by themselves. Likewise, free blacks were regularly part of the antebellum theater audience. Although there is no evidence that white citizens of Baltimore, Norfolk, and Richmond raised objections to free blacks patronizing the theaters, opponents of the theater were quick to proclaim that it had a debilitating effect on slaves. In November 1819 a writer in the *Richmond Commercial Compiler* voiced his fear that "the scenes which they witness, and the society with which they mix in the gallery" would demoralize servants. Another theater critic pointed out that slaves sometimes slipped off to performances without permission and purchased gallery seats with money that would have been more wisely spent in other ways.[13]

To underscore that the typical antebellum theater audience in Baltimore, Norfolk, and Richmond was mixed is not to say that there were no seating distinctions. Like theaters in other eastern cities, those in Baltimore, Norfolk, and Richmond usually were divided into three main areas: the boxes, the pit, and the gallery or galleries. Visitors who described theater audiences usually observed that the three areas housed three different social groups. Wealth and respectability were best represented in the boxes; middling or ordinary folks sat in the pit; and common folks and blacks, free or unfree, bought places in the galleries. During the antebellum period, box seats usually cost $0.75 to $1.00, while pit seats were $0.50, and gallery seats on long uncushioned benches without backs were $0.25. During this same period, gingham was about $0.11 per yard, an ordinary pair of shoes cost approximately $1.00, a blanket cost about $1.50, bacon was about $0.08 a pound, pork was $0.05 to $0.08 per pound, coffee was $0.22 per pound, and molasses was approximately $0.25 a gallon.[14]

The coexistence of status-based seating distinctions with the general mixed nature of the antebellum theater crowd epitomizes the ongoing tension in many nineteenth century amusements, especially those that had aristocratic precedents. Part of the tension expressed in the evolution of the theater resulted from attempts to alter this entertainment form that had been inherited from Europe to suit the pretensions of American democracy, especially Jacksonian democracy. Questions about behavior revealed the strain between allowing all expressions of taste—that, after all, was democracy—and maintaining some sort of order. The task, for those who were interested—and many were—was to create a uniquely American theater, with customs reflective of the young republic.

Another source of tension, which proved just as important in the creation of the theater as an amusement form, was the partiality of some of the audience toward aristocratic values. Although submerged during the first part of the century, the desire for order and hierarchy resurfaced in the late 1830s. Ironically, of course, this was during the time when Jacksonian democracy was at its height, suggesting that the renewed interest in hierarchy was at least in part reactionary.[15] During the first part of the century the tensions were expressed in a variety of ways, ranging from the arrangement of the space in the theater to questions about behavior and taste.

Blacks were the only spectators in the theater who were rigidly separated from the remainder of the audience in Baltimore, Norfolk, and Richmond. It is likely, given the sentiment of the time, that most white patrons would not have considered this a violation of democratic ideals. Occasionally there was outright exclusion; advertisements informed the public that there would be "No admittance for people of colour." At other times blacks were admitted only at special show times. When General Tom Thumb was in Richmond in 1851, advertisements announced that he would "hold levees at the African Church." Blacks, however, were only "admitted to the 3½ o'clock Levee on Saturday."[16] It was common practice for theaters to maintain separate galleries for "colored persons." Broadsides and advertisements for exhibitions, circuses, and theaters informed blacks that there were separate "places appropriated for their accommodation." Sometimes there was an additional gallery for mulattoes, but theaters made no official distinction between slaves and free blacks. By mid-century, however, some theaters boasted several "colored galleries" with price variations, suggesting that such a distinction probably existed. In 1853 advertisements for Baltimore's Holliday Street Theatre informed the public that a third tier had been remodeled for "the commodious accommodation of the reputable colored residents of Baltimore."[17]

The pit was home for a mixed group of people, ranging from artisans to journalists—a contrast with England, where theater critics sat in the pit and the common people filled the galleries. British traveler Henry Fearon registered his astonishment at some of the types he encountered in an American theater pit in 1817: "I went to the pit, concluding that, with an allowance for the difference of country, it would resemble the same department in an English establishment; but found it consisted of none in dress, manners, appearance, or habits above the order of our Irish bricklayers. . . . Here were men that, if in London, could hardly buy a pint of porter."[18] Another contemporary observed that the pit "is generally filled with young butchers, smart news-boys, stage-stricken poets, and penny-a-liners for the press."[19] American critics were not given special treatment or a special area. Rather, when they came, they sat among the audience—sometimes in boxes, sometimes in the pit. The pit in the American theater was another expression of American democracy; every person could be a critic.

Another attempt to adapt aristocratic forms to American democracy—to insure that early nineteenth-century theater was a public rather than a privileged place—is apparent in the way that box-seat tickets were marketed. Ordinarily these seats were sold for individual performances; that is, they were not sold or rented on a seasonal basis. Baltimore Theatre manager William B. Wood indicated that he often had refused offers to purchase boxes for the season because he thought that a permanent group of boxholders would set itself up as a privileged elite. Wood believed that the continuing success of the American theater depended on the public rather than powerful individuals or cliques. "In a country where the spirit of liberty is so fierce as in ours," he noted, "such a privilege would excite from an immense class a feeling of positive hostility" that would be the deathblow to the theater.[20]

The overall impact of the various modifications of traditional European theater practices was confusion—some critics would have said anarchy. Although the seating separated the various classes of the theater crowd, the early nineteenth-century audience's chief characteristic was its heterogeneity. Within the theater walls, the mixed crowd, despite seating distinctions, shared a common, and usually quite boisterous, culture. Until the late 1830s, theater audiences in Baltimore, Norfolk, and Richmond were, paradoxically, both separated and mixed. Despite separate seating, rowdiness was generalized throughout the audience. Often a wild and rollicking place, the theater seemed to encourage behavior that was unacceptable at home; enthusiasm cut across class lines.

In 1805, for example, newspaper correspondent Tommy Clod expressed disgust at the behavior of an unrestrained crowd in the Baltimore Theatre. First he railed at the "three Bucks behind me" who knocked 16-inch sticks together throughout the performance and "kept up such a confused babbling that I felt relief when her [the actress's] performance ended." Next he described the "segar" smokers in the building: "Of course, while they smoke, they cannot talk, but they are commonly attracted by those females who visit the upper boxes, then the uproar begins. They chatter with wonderful vigor, assume consequence, and act as madmen dead to all shame. They are commonly young men who live in stores, who desire to appear above the station which nature has allotted them."[21]

Although Tommy Clod was very irritated, he was not exaggerating. Crowds hooted and jeered, stomped and screamed, threw tomatoes, and sometimes sang along with the performers. Despite threats from managers and criticism from newspaper editorials, cigar smoking was a prevalent and potentially dangerous practice that persisted even after the Richmond Theatre fire. One newspaper contributor noted that management's attempts to block the use of tobacco inside the theater was fruitless as long as the disposition of the crowd favored smoking. "Our Bucks," he concluded, "delight in acting contrary to all rule and order."[22] The line between acting and reality was blurred. It was not uncommon for people from the audience to jump on the stage and interact with the make-believe characters.[23]

Sometimes, too, the performers responded with violence. In Norfolk in 1803 when a person in the gallery indicated dissatisfaction with a performance, the doorkeeper kicked him out of the gallery, and several of the performers attacked him. A correspondent to the newspaper suggested that the actors should "better exert themselves to merit attention by the *correctness of their performance,* than to silence censure by the strength of their arms, or their dexterity in the *pugilistic art.*"[24]

Other performers, either out of anger or frustration, stepped out of their roles and requested silence. Mostly however, they accepted the audience's activity and responded to the calls for incorporating requested songs or speeches, even if the crowd, as one Baltimore critic noted, usually would not stay quiet long enough to hear them. Satisfying the audience was no easy task. In 1826 when an actress identified as Miss Kelly was playing in Baltimore, she was forced to repeat all of her songs. The night, according to one critic, was "excessively warm," and the actress nearly fainted. Englishman Edward T. Coke described how irritated he became with a Baltimore audience in 1832 which "protracted the play in a most wearisome manner" by demanding so many encores.[25]

Disturbances often came from unlikely sources, as British traveler Charles William Janson discovered. Visiting the Baltimore Theatre in 1807, Janson was appalled by the behavior of a man who was seated behind him. The "vulgar, noisy, squat figure," Janson noted, attempted to be a critic for all those seated around him. He was extremely boisterous before the curtain rose, "uttering the most coarse and vulgar phrases, and ending each with a loud and hoarse laugh." He continued to voice his loud observations throughout the performance. Much to Janson's amazement, the man was not some common street misfit but a respectable bookseller. In his account of his trip, Janson told his readers: "I should not have descended to repeat such grossness, had not this man borne a nominal rank among those who are deemed respectable people; and what made this outrage more reprehensible, was, that one of the joint proprietors of the house, Reinagle, the musician, who presided in the orchestra during the performance, was a lodger in his house. Nor is this a singular instance of the kind; interruption by loud talking around you is common in all the American theatres."[26]

Thirty years after Janson's visit, Count Francesco Arese visited the Baltimore Theatre and was similarly disgusted by the crowd's behavior. Fearing that the loud "hisses might lead to other more concrete and violent demonstrations," Arese walked out before the program was finished.[27] In Richmond in 1847 a reviewer indicated that audience behavior was still less than satisfactory. "The majority of the audience," he observed, "show their impatience in loud talking and laughing, or melancholy yawns."[28]

Frequently, loud arguments broke out between or among members of the audience, creating additional problems for the harried managers. A letter to the *Federal Gazette* in 1815 indicated that quarrels were a serious problem and urged theater managers to take punitive action against those involved in scuffles. Sometimes the fights were triggered by differences of opinion about particular performances. At other times the disruption was totally unrelated to the show—a quarrel over a woman or someone's honor.[29] The two major theater riots that occurred in Baltimore during this period were reactions to statements that English actors made about Americans. In 1826 the Englishman Edmund Kean appeared at the Baltimore Theatre. The play went along well until Kean made his first speech, and then the decorum was shattered. Despite attempts to address and silence the clamoring audience, Kean could not make himself heard. Contemporaries noted that the boisterous elements were not confined to the galleries or pit; much of the disorder originated in the boxes.[30] In a situation reminiscent of the Kean riot, in 1853 another English actor, William Anderson, made some indiscreet statements about the "blarsted Yankees" while appearing at Baltimore's Adelphi Theatre. A few people purchased tickets to his next performance, but many more created an uproar by bursting into the theater after the show had begun and disrupting it. Anderson was ridiculed, despite his attempts to regain the audience's favor.[31]

The Kean and Anderson disturbances had a notorious parallel in the New York City Astor Place Riot of 1849, a disturbance that culminated a running feud between British actor Charles William Macready, a favorite of New York's elite, and American-born Edwin Forrest, a hero of the common people who played roles championing the masses. Posters around the city urged workingmen to express their opinions of Macready and his aristocratic ideas in a demonstration at the "AUTOCRATIC Opera House." Hearing of the proposed demonstration, a group of prominent New Yorkers, including Washington Irving and Herman Melville, urged Macready to adhere to his performance schedule so that there would be no acquiescence to the rowdies. The conflict between the two groups escalated into a full-blown riot that led to 31 deaths and at least 150 injuries.[32]

Despite the similarities, the Baltimore riots differed from the Astor Place Riot in one significant respect. The Kean and Anderson disturbances were expressions of faith in American democracy, rather than displays of contempt for aristocracy. That is, in each case the situation in the Baltimore theater was one in which the audience—a mixed crowd—united in opposition to an actor because of disparaging things he had said about Americans and the American way of life. Some of the women in the audience retired in disgust, but fighting did not break out between groups in the audience.[33] Possibly the difference reflects the times in which the riots occurred. By 1849 in New York the theaters were stratified by clientele; Astor Place was the resort of the elite. Distinctions among theaters had not, however, developed to any significant extent in Baltimore in 1826 or 1833. There were noticeable social gradations in the seating, but the classes did not patronize separate theaters. In both the Kean and Anderson riots the Baltimore crowds were intent on expressing solidarity against unappreciative British actors—an intent that exceeded any class lines and, for the moment, reaffirmed old beliefs in the absence of hard and fast class distinctions in America. Likewise, the rowdiness was spread throughout the mixed audiences.

Generally critics could not agree on who was responsible for theater disturbances, another indication that the behavior was spread throughout the audience. Even when there was a direct relationship between public disorder and some contributing factor, theater managers hesitated to circumscribe individual rights and put limits on public behavior. Bars and gambling dens in theater lobbies continued to operate, despite general acknowledgment that they were responsible for a great amount of the disruptive behavior, as well as for the vice that was connected with the theater. Clergyman C. B. Parsons labeled the bars and theater lobbies "the halls of abomination, the ante-chambers of sin and wickedness."[34] One Baltimore critic was particularly upset by the noise accompanying the sale and distribution of drinks during performances. "The sharp squirting noise of that concern," he observed, "is excessively annoying, so it is."[35] Nevertheless, excessive drinking and public drunkenness in theaters persisted in the antebellum period. Advertisements continued to include reference to barrooms, generally noting the barkeeper's name and the fact that the bar was well-stocked.[36]

Some suggested that the managers should exclude "persons conducting themselves improperly." Other critics pointed to specific areas of the theater that needed extra policing. A writer in the *Richmond Whig* in 1827 aimed his criticism at the gallery, urging the management to raise the prices, exclude the blacks, or hire police specifically to "check the overflowing of a riotous spirit among the coloured persons who nightly crowd there."[37] Another critic declared that the problems originated in

Public Behavior and the Theater

44

..

the pit, with the disagreeable crowd that gathered there. He suggested that to avoid a riot, the management should restrict the number of pit tickets to the number of pit seats.[38]

The bulk of the criticism was aimed, however, at the boxes, particularly the upper boxes. At first this appears incongruous; the box seats cost more than any other seats in the theater, and the more respectable people sat there. Baltimore Theatre manager William B. Wood was adamant, though, in locating the center of the disturbance in the boxes; he noted that in the second quarter of the century, while he was manager, "disorderly conduct was invariably confined to the boxes." During his long association with theaters in Philadelphia and Baltimore, he encountered only two instances when he had to remove people from the gallery or pit. He concluded that this was because "the unruly could stealthily mingle themselves with the respectable" in the boxes, "so as to escape the detection which a more concentrated effort would have engendered."[39] Frequently, of course, the respectable and the unruly were the same.

One group that mixed with the respectable in the boxes and often touched off disturbances was the prostitutes. Some theaters had a tier in the boxes that was almost exclusively patronized by prostitutes and their clients.[40] It appears that there was more prejudice against these women than any other group or class in the audience. Other women were especially annoyed. Attending theater productions in Norfolk at the beginning of the century often meant being surrounded by what the newspapers referred to as the "well-dressed damsels from Water Street, Bank Street, Lee's Wharf, etc." One Norfolk critic suggested that these women and the sailors who accompanied them ought to be relegated to the galleries so that the respectable playgoers would not be offended.[41] In his *History of the American Theatre* (published in 1832), William Dunlap said that the congregation of prostitutes in theaters was one of the major problems requiring regulation. He thought "that no female should come to a theatre unattended by a protector of the other sex, except such whose standing in society is a passport to every place," and urged managers to adopt such a rule.[42]

Managers often found themselves in a winless situation. If they admitted prostitutes, they were criticized by the local press; if they excluded prostitutes, they often lost not only the business of the prostitutes but that of the prostitutes' clientele. Some avoided a head-on collision with prostitutes and their supporters by advertising that women in general would not be admitted unless accompanied by a gentleman; this, however, was infrequent. An alternate approach to curbing disorderly behavior involved limiting the number of men in the section usually occupied by prostitutes or charging extra for any man who came by himself. The loss of such an important segment of the theater audience as prostitutes often meant financial difficulties. At the same time, prostitutes proved extremely adept in circumventing any regulations denying them access to the theater. In 1846 one clever woman, "well known to the police" in Baltimore, painted her face black "so as to obtain entrance to the boxes assigned to the colored folks" in the Roman Amphitheatre. She managed to gain admittance, but the police soon recognized her and sent her to spend "the remainder of the night upon the soft side of a plank at the Middle District Watch-House."[43]

Throughout the antebellum period theater managers and prostitutes were involved in struggles that helped shape the space in the theaters— the seating arrangements and location of bars—as well as the popular conception of the theater. Changes in the interior design of theaters in the 1850s—especially the addition of a parquette or parterre—served to create further space for prostitutes and their escorts or prospective clients. Clergyman C. B. Parsons called the parquette "a place of 'speckled birds'" and complained that the addition had created "a middle state in play-house morality betwixt the 'dress circle' and the 'third tier,'" where "the lady of liberal sentiments and her lord of negative responsibilities may sit together, without the requirement of a certificate of character."[44]

In her study of prostitution in American theaters, Claudia D. Johnson notes that the tension between managers and prostitutes presents a paradigm of the cultural history of Victorian America: "a secular art form is struggling for legitimacy against long-standing religious disapproval, while a stricter moral code is struggling against customary vice."[45] Once again, the struggle suggests the tensions that helped to define the American theater and theater behavior in the nineteenth century. The long-term outcome of the struggle over prostitution in theaters, at least in Baltimore, Norfolk, and Richmond, seems to have been a compromise that declared prostitution illegal but winked at individual cases, depending upon the social connections of those involved in the indiscretion. It was difficult for theater managers or the police to crack down on behavior that everyone but a few critics had grown accustomed to.

Managers typically responded to general complaints about behavior by issuing house rules, depending upon the public for help in enforcing them. Beginning in the 1820s, theater advertisements regularly included a statement indicating that "an efficient police" would be present to enforce good order. Offenders were threatened with legal action, and managers published rewards for apprehension of offenders. In 1829 the manager of Baltimore's Front Street Theatre advertised that anyone caught breaking the house rules not only would be prosecuted but also would be exposed through the newspapers.[46] William L. Maule, manager of the Richmond Theatre in the 1840s, posted broadsides delineating the "Rules and Regulations of the Richmond Theatre," prohibiting such things as smoking, loud conversation, and "whooping, hallooing, whistling, or other disorderly noises."[47] When it came to actual cases, however, very little was done to discourage the offenders from patronizing the theater, and rowdyism persisted in some theaters throughout the nineteenth century.

Managers hesitated to restrict admissions because they knew that full houses meant paid bills. It was necessary to attract large numbers to the theater, even if it was at the expense of quality in the entertainment. Theater manager William Dunlap voiced his embarrassment at some of the things he was forced to do to fill the cashbox and pay his stars. "Instead of studying to gain the approbation of the wise," he noted, he was forced to turn "his thoughts to the common methods of attracting the vulgar."[48] It was a question of the lowest common denominator. While the more cultured portion of the audience wanted Shakespeare and the classics, the larger portion wanted popular contemporary dramas. Dunlap regretted that the manager, in order to make ends meet, "was forced to neglect the few and cater to the many."[49]

Consequently, the managers' attempts to please the diverse interests in the early nineteenth-century audiences resulted in a motley program of various pieces and styles. Typically, the first play of the evening was a comedy, melodrama, or tragedy, which was followed by an intermission and a second play, usually a farce. Variations included one long play followed by two short pieces or two plays in one evening.[50] The bill for January 6, 1810, in the Richmond Theatre is typical of the mixed fare. John Howard Payne, who had just acted in Philadelphia, Baltimore, New York, and Boston, was engaged for seven nights. The program included

Coleman's opera MOUNTAINEERS
followed by a Pantomine Interlude called
HARLEQUIN HURRY-SKURRY, or
THE DEVIL AMONG THE TRADES-FOLK
to which is added the Comic Farce
HIGH LIFE BELOW THE STAIRS[51]

Early in the century, American crowds, like their European counterparts, enjoyed performances that featured wars and battles, especially if
there was sword combat. At the same time, the introduction of an exotic
live animal, such as an elephant, also drew favorable response. Indian
plays were very popular between 1830 and 1840, following the success
of John Augustus Stone's *Metamora; or, The Last of the Wampanoags.* The
1840s and 1850s saw the rise in popularity of tableaux vivants, set pieces
(usually historical) in which the actors remained motionless and speech-
less, as though in a painting.[52] Perhaps the popularity of this style in the
late antebellum period reflects the uneasy peace between the sections and
the fears that the peace might soon be shattered. The tableaux vivants
allowed time to stand still. Southerners would dwell on the historical
events to which they had so greatly contributed without thinking about
the ways in which the slave system had perverted the ideals of the
democratic republic. Northern audiences could focus on the same historical tableaux vivants without having to carry the ideals through to their
ultimately divisive conclusion.

On the eve of the Civil War, as events moved the sections further
apart, there was a corresponding increase in interest in plays with
political overtones. In Northern theaters this frequently meant that
plays were blatantly abolitionist. In the South, political themes were not
as prominent; but slavery, when included, was presented as a benign
institution. Baltimore theater reflected its geographical situation and
the city's divided opinion over the slavery issue. The original Little Eva
recalled that before the Civil War her father's company presented *Uncle
Tom's Cabin* as far south as Baltimore without meeting any opposition.
During the same period Baltimore audiences also saw *The White Slave of
England,* a burlesque of *Uncle Tom's Cabin* that ridiculed many abolitionist premises.[53]

Sectional divisions, however, did not completely sever the ties between Southern theaters and Northern theatrical centers. A comparison of plays that were popular in Baltimore and Richmond with those most popular in New York, Philadelphia, Alexandria, and Washington indicates that there was little difference in what was presented. Of forty plays presented in Philadelphia before their Richmond opening, eighteen were in Richmond within a year of their first performance in Philadelphia. Many of the same actors performed in the same plays in Baltimore, Richmond, Norfolk, New York, Philadelphia, Charleston, Washington, and other American cities—frequently within a short period of time. Theater management provided one further tie between sections. Often the managers were as transient as the stars, renting a theater in Philadelphia for a season, for example, and then moving on to another theater in Baltimore or Richmond.[54]

Walking the managerial tightrope required great skill. Something as simple as setting ticket prices involved major decisions and required a manager to anticipate his patrons' response. Lower prices, for example, did not always increase attendance. As Baltimore Theatre manager William Wood discovered, lower prices sometimes kept the more respectable people away.[55] Part of the manager's problems stemmed from the crowds' desires to see stars perform, and stars cost a theater a high percentage of its gross receipts. The stars were mainly European performers whose reputations had preceded them across the Atlantic via the press. Oddly enough, the devotion to stars seems, once again, to reflect the democratic nature of the antebellum theater. In a culture where many theatergoers were not knowledgeable about drama—and were not expected to be—stars, rather than playwrights or particular plays, were the theater. (The exceptions, of course, were playwrights such as Shakespeare who were also famous.) Managers promoted stars as commodities that all could consume. Because of their prominence as theatrical centers, Baltimore and Richmond both attracted the major star performers as they traveled the theater circuit from North to South. Norfolk, although not so prominent, also got its share of stars; most traveled by way of Norfolk to other Southern towns such as Wilmington, North Carolina, or Charleston, South Carolina.

Editorials praised managers for importing "star after star." A partial list of performers in Baltimore, Norfolk, and Richmond reads like a who's who of nineteenth-century acting. John Howard Payne, Tyrone Power, Laura Keene, Edwin Booth, Mary Derlin, Ida Vernon, Charles

Kean, Edmund Kean, the Chapman sisters, Edwin Forrest, Joseph Jefferson, Charlotte Cushman, and Adelaide Neilson were a few of the stars that audiences clamored to see. Junius Brutus Booth made his American debut on a Richmond stage in 1821, a fact that Richmond playgoers remembered throughout the century.[56] Public enthusiasm for stars often got out of hand, as the response to German ballerina Fanny Elssler indicates. After an Elssler performance at the Baltimore Theatre in 1840, an exuberant crowd unhitched the horses from her carriage and drew the star from the theater to her hotel themselves. Later, at her arrival for a stint in Richmond, a group of prominent citizens met and escorted her to her hotel with a brass band.[57]

Outside the theater, as the Elssler example suggests, the relationship between performers and the community was usually very amicable. For every critic who pointed to a star's eccentricities, there was usually another who came to the star's defense, as well as to the defense of the theater in general. John Pendleton Kennedy emphasized the rapport between the audience and the players: "When our players came, with their short seasons, their three nights in the week, and their single company, they were received as public benefactors, and their stay was a period of carnival."[58] The usual favorable response to benefits—those performances given solely to make money for a particular star or manager—also suggests the general support for stars and the theater in Baltimore, Norfolk, and Richmond.

The star system and its consequences were not, however, with critics. One writer deplored the "scandalous" behavior of the crowd after the Elssler concert, noting the extent to which audience enthusiasm for a star could exceed the bounds of decency. Other critics thought star worship was a terrible misappropriation of values. When John Howard Payne acted in Richmond for eight nights in 1810 and received $1,710, a communication in the newspaper compared this with the $200 that a judge of the Court of Appeals received annually. Theater manager Wood thought that ruinous seasons in Baltimore were caused by the exorbitant salaries demanded by stars. Improvements to theater structures or additions of nonacting personnel often had to be postponed because of the primacy of paying the stars.

There was also the problem of creating a viable American theater with competent and respected American performers. This was difficult to achieve as long as American theater audiences preferred European stars to unknown American actors—a preference to which visitors such as Frances Trollope and James S. Buckingham attested.[59] Moreover, the presentation of many English plays in America only a few months after their London openings further suggests the American theatergoers' preference for what had already been critically acclaimed.[60] Again, this presents an interesting irony; while the democratic nature of the theater helped to stoke the appetite for stars, the mass appeal of European stars impeded the development of a uniquely American, democratic theater, with American plays and performers.

The general heterogeneity of the theater audience remained a powerful factor shaping the theater in Baltimore, Norfolk, and Richmond until the middle of the century. As the century progressed, additional theaters were built, particularly in growing urban areas where the populations could support a variety of amusements. The greater number of theaters meant more entertainment choices for audiences. In the long run, this change also led to a transformation of the theater, a change that Tyrone Power sensed in 1836 when he was acting at the Front Street Theatre in Baltimore. Power wrote that he discerned the beginning of some distinctions between the city's theaters. "I have discovered," he noted, "that the *people* are with *us*; the 'Holiday' being considered the aristocratic house, and 'the Front,' being, indeed, the work of an opposition composed of the sturdy democracy of the good city."[61]

In Baltimore and Richmond distinctions among the various theaters began to appear in the late 1830s, when the number of theaters had increased to the point that, in order to compete with each other, they began offering a variety of alternative programs. Instead of one theater that presented a variety of entertainments in one evening's showing, each of the various theaters began to specialize in presenting one type of entertainment. Distinctions in Norfolk theaters occurred a little later— in the next decade—primarily because the population had to grow before it could support a wide variety of programs. By 1830 four theaters operated in Baltimore—the Front, the Adelphi, the Holliday, and Peale's. The avid playgoer, as theater historian Alonzo May noted, "could regale on Tragedy, Drama, revel in the witticisms of Comedy, enjoy the absurdities of Farce or laugh at the antics of the Clown, and all in one week!"[62]

Proprietors advertised the particular kinds of presentations that their theaters had assumed as specialities. The owner of the Vaudeville Pavilion that opened in Baltimore in 1839, for example, announced that it was designed specifically "for the production of Vaudevilles, Operas and Spectacles."[63] Upper-class playgoers began to patronize certain theaters, while the middle and lower classes went to others. The divisions were not always precise, but the trend was established. The Holliday Street Theatre, in fact, maintained its position as Baltimore's leading theater for the remainder of the century. Except for a short interval when it was being rebuilt, the Richmond Theatre (formerly the Marshall) was the most prestigious theater in Richmond.[64]

By the middle of the century, observers were commenting on the noticeable differences in audience behavior in the various theaters. Writers contrasted the decorum observed in the Baltimore's Holliday, Norfolk's Opera House, or the Richmond with the uproar that filled some of the lesser theaters. The public gradually began to connect particular theaters with specific classes. For the most part, once a theater became known as a resort of the lower class, it had that reputation for the rest of its existence. Similarly, theaters that had traditionally catered to the upper class usually continued in this vein, at least as long as the theater manager could make a profit by doing so. A reputation of exclusiveness attracted aspiring middle-class citizens as well as upper-class patrons. Attempting to avoid becoming a resort of lowlifes or rowdies, some new theaters opened with promises of strict order. The management of the Continental Opera House in Baltimore went so far as to ban the admission of youths, noting that they were often responsible for the misbehavior in the theater—an assumption that the evidence does not always warrant.[65]

Miscalculations or changes in management and emphasis sometimes affected the quality of a theater and, subsequently, the type of audience it attracted. In the 1850s, for example, the *Baltimore American* praised Peale's Theatre for its "good order and comfort." The theater was known for its high-quality performances given to substantial audiences.[66] Peale's went through many changes, however, as it passed through a succession of proprietors. George Kunkle purchased it in September 1861, renamed it Kunkle's Ethiopian Opera House, and specialized in minstrel shows. It continued to decline, both in terms of the entertainment it offered and the crowds it attracted. Eventually, as Baltimore historian J. Thomas Scharf noted, it "became a disreputable place, with its brazen, painted women and wine-room." On May 9, 1866, a man was killed there in a shoot-out.[67]

Wild arguments culminating in gunfire were not uncommon in the lower-class theaters. Increasingly, as the urban areas evolved, the lower-class theaters were in less reputable sections of the city. Meredith Janvier's description of sneaking off to a "Second Class Theatre" (as he labeled it) in the late 1860s suggests the atmosphere:

> Kernan's Monumental we called "the Bridge," and I stole off to matinees, being doubtless afraid to visit this part of town after dark, as it was beyond Market Space, a scene of fights and marauding. Drinks were served at the "Bridge" throughout the performance by darky waiters, who called "Beer, cigars and soda." The seats were covered with cream-tinted oilcloth, doubtless to protect them from spilled liquors. The gallery gods, two-thirds of them news-boys and bootblacks, sang and whistled the chorus to every song, and order was preserved by a man with a red moustache. He rapped on the wall with a rattan cane.[68]

The description of the developments in the theater are significant for several reasons. First, of course, the number of commentators who noticed the differences suggests that theaters were distinguished by the composition of their audiences and that there really were major differences in audience behavior in the various theaters. More important, however, is what these developments say about prevailing beliefs about public behavior. Sometime in the 1840s, some patrons in theater audiences became concerned about maintaining decorum. Either something important happened to turn a portion of the old mixed theater audience away from rowdiness, or the feelings were always there, just temporarily hidden in the glorification of democratic habits. The rapidity of the transformation suggests that there may have been a combination of both. For those who were interested, the expansion in theater choices provided the opportunity to separate and to avoid unruly crowds.

This inference is supported by a look at reactions to developments in minstrelsy in the mid-nineteenth century. The minstrel show evolved from song and dance skits to more substantial comedies, before degenerating into bawdy female minstrel shows that appealed to a vulgar audience. In the 1840s minstrelsy had an amazing appeal for all classes.

Minstrel troupes performed at most of the major entertainment halls in
Baltimore, from the Baltimore Theatre to Raymond's Circus Arena, to
audiences that ran the spectrum from slaves to genteel ladies. In fact, in
1843 one Ethiopian show at the Assembly Rooms had to be extended
because of the large crowds of the city's elite, especially women, who had
turned out to see it.[69]

More and more, however, minstrel shows reflected the close interaction between the performers and the vociferous elements in the audience
that they attempted to satisfy. Minstrel troupes performed less frequently in legitimate theaters and more often in halls established specifically for minstrelsy. The shows provided a choice between popular and
formal performances and were an option that the upper class was increasingly less likely to take. In Baltimore in the 1850s the troupes
usually appeared at Apollo Hall, while Richmond shows generally were
staged at Metropolitan Hall; neither of these halls was a first-rate theater.
The Ethiopian Opera House that George Kunkel opened in 1861 in
Baltimore rapidly degenerated into a disreputable place.[70]

One final development, which ultimately made minstrelsy unacceptable to both the middle and upper classes, was the opening of female
minstrel shows. These shows offered the possibility of viewing partially
dressed women and appealed mostly to crowds of rowdy men and boys.
When discussing her job, one female minstrel noted that the "main
thing is shape." All the show girls had to do was "put on their costumes
and let the jays look at them." She concluded: "We give a tough show,
draw tough houses, and have a tough time."[71] Describing a crowd
gathered in Norfolk to view Madame Rente's Female Minstrels, a reporter noted that the house "was packed" with "an audience composed
entirely of men and boys" who filled the hall with "yells of applause and
boisterous laughter."[72]

The Civil War created numerous problems for the theater, including
strains on management and performers, and inflation caused ticket prices
to skyrocket. A study of the Confederate theater in Richmond indicates,
however, that in the long run the war did not alter the trends that had
already been set in motion. While battles were raging all around,
sometimes within a few miles, the Richmond theaters played on. They
were often the last public institutions to close when Union troops
marched into town.[73] In response to a request from the army, the
theaters did close for a week in June 1862 after the bloody battle of Seven

Public Behavior and the Theater

54
. . .

Pines (Fair Oaks) on the outskirts of Richmond. They remained open throughout the summer, however, even through the Seven Days battles.

Numerous articles in the *Southern Punch* encouraged the authorities to allow the theaters to remain open, noting that this would give the North the impression that the South, particularly the Southern capital, was not panicking. One article, for example, suggested that nervous Confederate officials should emulate the calm found in theater audiences: "One of the most refreshing sights to be seen is a merry, contented audience, waiting upon a theatrical presentation during these thunderous times. There we find an absence of that foolish alarm which should be copied by some officials of the Confederacy—proof positive that laughing ladies, jubilant men, among the latter numbers of convalescent soldiers, have not the shadow of an idea that Grant and Butler will get nearer to Richmond than to see its tall steeples from a seat in the basket of a balloon."[74] The Confederate government rescinded closure orders, and interest in theatricals increased as the war progressed. The theater served as an outlet for patriotic expression as well as escape. Even the Union army's triumphant entry and takeover of Richmond did not significantly affect the theater. The performance scheduled for April 3, 1865, was canceled, but the theater reopened the next night, after issuing special invitations to Union officials.[75]

The three main theaters in Confederate Richmond, the Richmond Varieties (formerly the Richmond Theatre), Metropolitan Hall, and the Richmond Lyceum, concentrated in different areas. The Varieties presented legitimate drama, Metropolitan Hall featured dramatic lecturers, and the Lyceum offered light comedies and farces.[76] Nevertheless, one consequence of the war situation, particularly Richmond's position as capital, was that the audiences were more heterogeneous than they had been in the fifteen to twenty years leading up to the war. Genteel ladies and gentlemen mixed with the numerous politicians, soldiers, and transients who gathered in town. Richmond Theatre manager John Hill Hewitt noted that he had to lower his theatrical standards and present some second-rate military dramas because of the number of soldiers in the crowd. Drinking at the theater became a major problem. At one point a *Richmond Dispatch* editor warned that drinking and the disturbances it produced would force respectable people to stop attending the theater.[77]

Although the war slowed and occasionally reversed the trend toward stratification of the theaters, it did not alter the course. Upper-class citizens did sometimes mix with the crowds at a public theater, but they also attended private theatricals produced solely for their own amusement. Generally these productions were given at private homes for invited guests; often they were followed by supper. One man who attended several of the private shows noted that the audience usually included officers of the Confederacy as well as prominent Richmond citizens.[78]

The trend toward stratification continued in the postwar period. The upper class patronized opera, serious drama, or polite comedy, while ordinary citizens attended theaters that featured less refined offerings. An opera craze in Richmond in the late forties and early fifties revived among the upper class after the war. One Richmond woman noted that despite postwar hardships, the elite made every effort to attend: "Indeed it is so unfashionable not to go to the opera that people don't like to acknowledge that they have so little taste as to stay away and the Ladies are buying opera cloaks and opera hats who are not able to pay their debts, but so the world goes, and every day you hear of failures, and a general despondency among all classes but still these people must be excited in one way or another."[79] Opera productions, usually Italian or German, ran for several days or a week at a time. The press indicated that the crowds were "refined and appreciative," of "fashionable society," or "of that character which insures the success of an operatic production."[80]

In Norfolk in April 1869, the Norfolk Opera House was advertising "THE BEAUTIFUL AND GIFTED CHAPMAN SISTERS" for refined audiences, while the Norfolk Varieties was advertising "SONGS, DANCES, BURLESQUES, NEGRO ECCENTRICITY" for "STRANGERS! CITIZENS! ANYBODY!" The Varieties further assured its image by advertising itself as the "RESORT OF THE MASSES."[81] Obviously, the tension between democracy and hierarchy had not been resolved in a simple manner. As an amusement form, the theater was democratic to the extent that it offered a variety of choices to a large segment of the population. Nevertheless, the stratification of theaters according to the social status of the patrons led to a hierarchy of sorts. Despite attempts at regulation, rowdiness continued in some theaters. At the other end of the spectrum, aristocratic pretensions found an outlet in theaters that catered to the elite.

There are many possible explanations for the way the nineteenth-century theater evolved once there was more opportunity for theater and program choices. One, of course, would have to account for differences in taste, the product of a complex mixture of things such as family background, education, and economics. Fads also influenced theater choices; some people chose their amusements because of what was current or what their friends were doing. At the same time, it is obvious that some middle- and upper-class people preferred socializing with people who were like them, maintaining a distance from those below. The stratification of theaters afforded them an opportunity to do so. Those who considered themselves upper class, in particular, appreciated the value of maintaining a tightly knit elite group so that they and their children would be more likely to socialize and marry within class ranks. Finally, it is obvious that many upper-class citizens chose to patronize a theater based on the status that attendance there might confer. The stratification of theaters suggests that some people continued to long for and support hierarchy despite—or perhaps because of—the emphasis on democracy and democratic institutions in the antebellum period.

Chapter Four

Social Control and
the Decline of Gambling
and Horse Racing

.·. **"G**aming," wrote French visitor La Rochefoucauld-Liancourt at the end of the eighteenth century, "is the ruling passion of the Virginians: at pharo, dice, billiards, at every imaginable game of hazard, they lose considerable sums. Gaming-tables are publicly kept in almost every town, and particularly at Richmond." He noted that despite a law that prohibited games of hazard and wagers on horse races or cockfights, "the greater number of those who enacted the law—of the present legislators, the justices of the peace, and the other magistrates—are assiduous in their attendance at those feats of gambling."[1]

Other sources support the Frenchman's account. A committee appointed to study gambling in Richmond in 1833 noted that there was "a conflict between the sentiments of the community and our legislative enactments." Visit any gambling house, it concluded, and you would find "legislators—even it has been said, the administrators of justice—the fashionable, the honorable, the educated: and they talk over the next day, their various fortunes at the faro table, with a businesslike sobriety, or a fashionable nonchalance."[2] The situation was similar in Baltimore and Norfolk. During the first half of the nineteenth century, gambling-oriented competitions such as cockfights, card games, billiards, horse racing, and games of chance had a broad following. The only significant exception was prizefighting, which was followed throughout the century mostly by what the *Baltimore American* termed "a certain class" or "roughs."[3] Although prizefighting was illegal, underground notices alerted people to upcoming pugilistic encounters.

Visitors noted that while residents of the upper South did not drink as much as their fellow Southerners, they made up for that moderation by their profligate gambling. Patrons played in taverns that had special rooms equipped for various games. Even Norfolk, as visitor Francis Baily recorded, had twelve of these as early as 1796. Baily also noted that everyone was admitted to the billiard tables, cockfights, or card games, "some of them not of the most remarkable caste; but still, *when it comes to their turn,* they *will* have their game, notwithstanding there may be some of the first people in the country waiting to play."[4]

Some who thought it sinful to attend the theater had no such misgivings about an afternoon around a cockpit. Similarly, bullbaitings, although not as common, were held in public places—in front of Richmond's Eagle Hotel, for example. Visitors observed that the crowds that gathered to watch and wager were composed of the "respectable" as well as the "refuse" of the city.[5] In 1804 a Baltimore critic attributed the lack of support for a benefit given for and starring Joseph Jefferson to the "gaming and dissipation . . . so prominent among the fashionable class of our citizens."[6]

When travelers attempted to account for the general dissoluteness that they claimed to see, they offered a variety of explanations. Some thought that it was endemic to the American character, while others blamed the government-sanctioned lotteries for setting a bad example. A more popular explanation centered on the nature of the state. Republican institutions, noted one visitor, tended to generalize the "luxury and licentiousness" that monarchical governments gave to the upper classes.[7] On the surface, that seemed to be the case; until the 1830s, democracy gave equal opportunity to participate in gambling ventures; disorder reigned supreme. One thing that was not so readily apparent to visitors, however, was the way the upper class controlled that disorder. Unlike the theater, where a rowdy looseness prevailed in all crowds until the elite withdrew and established stricter rules of decorum in elite theaters, gambling and horse racing appeared loose but usually were tightly controlled in fairly subtle ways related to deference. The elite withdrew when they could no longer maintain this control.

The first indication that control was slipping away from the elite was the growing significance of professional gamblers. By the 1830s professional gamblers, many transient, had organized gambling houses in most of the major cities of the United States. Usually the professional purchased an interest in some established gambling rooms, paying $1,000 or more plus part of the profits. These resorts, known in the trade as "Skinning-Houses," served their clientele elegant suppers and gave them liquor and cigars. Such houses opened in Baltimore and Richmond in the mid-1830s. At the same time, those who did not want to participate with the general crowd could play in private rooms, often in hotels. According to John O'Connor, a professional gambler who worked the East Coast during the nineteenth century, these elegantly furnished "genteel gambling-rooms" became very popular in the 1830s. Professional gamblers also set up tables for short stands at taverns and maintained booths at the racecourses during the racing seasons. They traveled to the Virginia springs for the summer season and usually were successful in emptying the pocketbooks of numerous players. By the 1840s billiards also fell prey to professional gamblers or "sharpers."[8]

Developments in horse racing in the first half of the nineteenth century were intertwined with what was happening in public gambling, especially because gambling was an important adjunct of the race day. After a slight downturn in 1810, horse racing revived in Baltimore, Norfolk, and Richmond, with the establishment of new racetracks. The Maryland and Virginia courses, in fact, had national reputations. In Baltimore the interest was such that the *American Turf Register,* a racing journal with a national readership, was established there in 1829.[9] Area residents also subscribed to the *Spirit of the Times,* a sportsman's journal published in New York. This was not particularly surprising, because many horsemen from the Upper South raced their horses at Northern tracks. The correspondence of prominent people from the Richmond area suggests that horse breeding and racing sometimes took precedence over politics. Even fashionable ladies enjoyed betting a glove or so on a favorite horse.[10]

In 1809 British visitor Anne Ritson captured the nature of the Southern racing field in a poem, which included a depiction of the mixed nature of the crowd:

> With gentle, simple, rich, and poor,
> The race-ground soon is cover'd o'er;
> Negroes the gaming spirit take,
> And bet and wager ev'ry stake;
> Males, females, all, both black and white,
> Together at this sport unite.[11]

The Decline of Gambling and Horse Racing

Politicians, prominent planters and merchants, and ladies and gentlemen of town and country viewed the same race as the servants, journeymen, and apprentices. They did so from different vantage points, however, and afterwards went to separate functions. Racecourses in Baltimore, Norfolk, and Richmond were operated by elite private jockey clubs; club members financed the organization with dues, usually $25 per year. This was a fairly common practice in the South; Charleston's elite controlled racetracks there through private jockey clubs. Although anyone could attend race day, entry in the races was rarely open to nonmembers. The clubs held elaborate parties and dinners for members and guests and made extensive provisions for members' comfort. The clubhouse of Tree Hill Course near Richmond had sleeping quarters for fifty members, a dining hall that seated several hundred, and a separate stand for ladies. A notice in the *Richmond Enquirer* in 1813 underscored the value of club membership; "A Dinner will be provided by the Proprietor the day of the Jockey Club Race, for the members of the Club, to be paid out of the subscription to the Club, agreeable to the resolution of the Club at their last Fall Meeting." [12]

While the upper class sat in the club's race stand, the remainder of the crowd spread out throughout the race grounds. While jockey club members ate in the club's dining hall or returned to town for dinner parties, everyone else ate at the booths that were set up on the field for selling liquor and food. These booths were patronized by a motley crowd—or, as the *American Turf Register* of May 1837 observed, "a most awful phalanx of every shade of colour." [13] The booths at the Fairfield track outside of Richmond were moved to a distant part of the field in 1813 because groups gathering at them were annoying other patrons. At the Baltimore course in 1825 Joseph Pickering found "a great number of men and boys of the working classes, and apprentices, throwing quoits, bowling, shooting at marks, pitch and hustle, &c. and gambling in the booths." [14] A general rowdiness prevailed, but for the most part, the upper class still controlled the important aspects of the race day—the races and most of the gambling.

Although racing in Baltimore, Norfolk, and Richmond remained popular in the 1830s and 1840s, there were signs of decline. Jockey clubs passed more rules against unlawful gaming and general disorder, including discharging guns on the racecourse. [15] Jockey clubs disbanded, and the composition of the crowd changed. By the mid-1850s horse racing had suffered a major decline, which was attributed to its close association with gambling. By 1860 the races, as Richmonder Samuel Mordecai recorded, were "chiefly in possession of a class, termed in softened phrase, 'sporting characters,' in the same way that negro-traders are called 'speculators.' Exclusive of the racing, the field presents a scene of the lowest gambling and dissipation."[16] Race days were no longer as popular among the upper class, and the courses, as a consequence, lost financial support. By the time of the Civil War, popular opinion no longer gave unequivocal sanction to public gambling. Legislation brought an end to public lotteries, and respectable citizens no longer wished to be seen patronizing such things as cockfights or public gaming rooms.

Various people have offered explanations for the shifting attitudes toward gambling and racing. Mid-nineteenth-century critics of gambling stressed the way amicable eighteenth-century tavern games had evolved into scenes of rough behavior, even bloodshed, by the 1830s and 1840s. They tried to convince their contemporaries that the antebellum period somehow spawned the corruption that they connected with all forms of gaming, and they pointed to the increasing number of professional gamblers as a special source of disorder. In reality, however, bloodshed had been fairly common in all gambling circles since the eighteenth century. Arguments over cheating quite commonly exploded into duels or outright murder. In 1806 in Norfolk, when a gambler broke the bank at one of the faro dens, the owners charged him with cheating. He responded by stabbing them both to death with a stiletto.[17]

Historians generally have attributed the decline of racing in the 1840s to a perception that it was tainted by its connection with gambling. In *The Rise of the City, 1878–1898,* Arthur M. Schlesinger stated the commonly held belief that racing failed to retain universal acceptance "because of the evils of betting and fraud which ordinarily attended it."[18] Similarly, in his study of nineteenth-century sports in New Orleans, Dale Somers linked racing's decline to a strong antigambling crusade.[19] These historians also noted stronger attempts to curtail gambling in the 1840s. Advertisements for hotels or resorts commonly noted that gambling would not be tolerated. State and local leaders passed a large amount of antigambling legislation in the decades before the Civil War.

A close look at gaming legislation in Baltimore, Norfolk, and Rich-

The Decline of Gambling and Horse Racing

mond suggests, however, that most legislation during the antebellum period was intended to eliminate those professionals who were profiting from the system, rather than to attack gambling in general. Several laws passed in Virginia in 1779 and 1792 were aimed primarily at the keepers of gambling rooms. An act of January 18, 1819, reduced into one all preceding acts. According to this law, keepers or exhibitors of gaming tables were subject, upon conviction, to hard labor and imprisonment for one to two years and a fine not exceeding $500. "Lewd and dissolute persons" who had no visible support but gaming could be brought before two justices of the peace and required to post bond as security for good behavior for twelve months. Players or bettors, meanwhile, were fined only $20 and security for good behavior for one year; this part of the law was intended not so much to punish the players as to prevent them from falling "in company with lewd, idle and dissolute persons, who have no other way of maintaining themselves but by gaming." Simple wagers or bets on horse races, cockfights, or other games were declared void, but there was no penalty if the money was repaid to the loser.[20] By an act of 1828 the maximum sentence was decreased to eight months, but the maximum fine was increased to $800, depending on the discretion of the jury.[21]

A committee appointed to devise means of suppressing gambling in Richmond in 1833 underscored the extent to which the intent of previous legislation was to stop professionals. According to this committee, the purpose of gambling laws was "to break up the haunts of professional gamblers and black-legs, who opened their faro tables in Richmond, and at all the public watering places, to the great injury of the unsuspecting and unwary, who were cheated of their substance, and often seduced to their ruin."[22] The committee noted that no one would give the justices of the peace enough evidence on which to base a warrant. This was not because of any great sympathy with the keepers of gambling houses but because potential witnesses feared that they might also implicate friends and acquaintances who were players. To rectify the situation, the committee recommended that attorneys have subpoena power. It also recommended stiffer penalties for keepers or exhibitors of gaming tables. The committee specified that the distinction between punishments for the player and exhibitor should be retained, because the two did not display the same degree of guilt and depravity.[23]

The maximum sentence for keepers or exhibitors was increased again

by a law of 1849, to twelve months, and the maximum fine was raised to
$1,000. A person convicted of using fraudulent means to acquire some-
thing from another person could be jailed for one year and fined not less
than five times the value of the thing that was won. At the same time,
the fine for players or bettors at public places was raised just $10 to $30
plus security for good behavior for one year.[24]

Another indicator that the concern was professional gamblers and disorder rather than gambling in general was the stipulation that players or
bettors at games that were in private places were not liable if their
winnings or losses did not exceed $20. By a law of 1852 blacks and
whites who gambled with blacks were excepted from this distinction;
regardless of their winnings or losses, they were still guilty of a misde-
meanor, whether the gaming was in public or private.[25]

Legislation in Maryland during the antebellum period also was directed against those making their livelihoods by gambling rather than
against the players. Most Maryland laws included specific penalties for
possession of gambling devices. As early as 1797 a law was passed to stop
exhibitors from carrying "from one public place to another in this state
certain gambling machines or inventions, calculated to deceive and
defraud the innocent and unguarded." An act of 1826 set a penalty of
from $1,000 to $2,000 and imprisonment of up to twelve months for
keepers of gaming tables or banks or for "strolling about the country
from place to place, and deriving a support and maintenance chiefly from
gambling."[26] An act of 1842 set a fine of $100 for each gaming table
that was kept, while players were still fined $20; an act of 1853 increased
the penalties for keepers of gaming houses and operators of gaming
devices, but the fine for players was not changed.[27]

Lottery legislation in both Virginia and Maryland during the first half
of the nineteenth century also was designed to regulate lotteries and
prevent unscrupulous dealers from taking advantage of other citizens.
The law in Virginia, for example, drew a distinction between public and
private lotteries, treating the latter as unlawful gaming "not because
lotteries were esteemed to be essentially and necessarily immoral, but
because the unrestrained privilege of *private* lotteries was capable of being
so abused."[28] Domestic lotteries were authorized by law until 1851 in
Baltimore and were held as late as 1859; in Virginia they were legal until
1852 and continued for some years after that time.[29] Visiting Richmond
in 1856, Thomas Ewbank indicated that in contrast to the absence of

The Decline of Gambling and Horse Racing

lotteries in Northern cities, lotteries were still flourishing in the Old Dominion. He noted that most Richmonders assumed that men wanted to gamble and lotteries were a means of directing the general desire into "beneficial public channels."[30] The same general gambling spirit—the desire to acquire something for nothing—was also apparent in the rapid spread of California gold fever to eager young men from Baltimore, Norfolk, and Richmond. Tales of sacks of gold and uncommon wealth sparked many to make the westward trek in the late 1840s and early 1850s.[31]

Historian T. H. Breen has analyzed the way Virginia planters unconsciously preserved social tranquility and class cohesion in the seventeenth century through gaming relationships. "By wagering on cards and horses," writes Breen, the planters "openly expressed their extreme competitiveness, winning temporary emblematic victories over their rivals without thereby threatening the social tranquility of Virginia."[32] Generally the betting was between men—or occasionally women—of the same social class. The gentry did not consider it proper to wager with the lower classes, although subordinates often had their own wager pools. Although anyone could attend as a spectator, horse racing was more exclusive than most games because the race field was usually limited to planter-owned horses, and the owners usually rode in the quarter-horse contests themselves.[33] The exclusiveness supported the gentry's social dominance. Breen concludes that "these colorful, exclusive contests helped persuade subordinate white groups that gentry culture was desirable, something worth emulating; and it is not surprising that people who conceded the superiority of this culture readily accepted the gentry's right to rule."[34]

In the seventeenth and eighteenth centuries, as Breen's study suggests, gaming derived from and, in turn, helped maintain a fairly rigid social stratification. Even in the early part of the nineteenth century, an afternoon spent wagering at the local racetrack was entertaining and, at the same time, valuable in proclaiming the status of the upper class. By the 1830s, however, this was no longer the case. Professional gamblers had usurped the role previously undertaken by the upper class. Professional gambler John O'Connor reminisced that the fall racing season, from August through mid-November, was one of his busiest periods. Noting that gamblers on the race field often had problems with other gamblers who set up games outside the race gates, O'Connor recounted how one enterprising professional, viewing the competition as "an infringement on his privileges," sent armed men to break up games in progress outside the track.[35]

Given the general disposition toward gambling, it is hard to document a strong antigambling crusade, and even harder to determine the reasons for the declining support of public gambling. Some historians have argued that the impact of the Second Great Awakening in the South was responsible for a profound change in character, as well as a reform orientation that led people to see gambling in a new—evil—light. Recent studies of the impact of evangelical Protestantism on the Old South, however, suggest that this was not the case. In *The Great Revival* John Boles, for example, underscores the way in which the thrust of the Southern revival was vastly different from that of its Northern counterpart. The new popular religion in the Old South was "individualistic, conversion-oriented, provincial, and anti-institutional." Ministers aimed to convert individual sinners, not to transform society. Consequently, Boles notes, "the evangelical groups in the South took comparatively little notice of political and social matters." While there were religious charity organizations, there was never anything like the reform movements and social gospel that had developed in New York's Burned-Over District.[36]

Another reason that has been offered to explain the change in attitudes is women's disapproval of gaming and racing. As Anne Firor Scott has noted, Southern women had much more influence over day-to-day society than their position in that patriarchial society would suggest.[37] Racing proprietors understood the value of having women's approval and attempted to win support from women by establishing special ladies' sections and offering an occasional ladies' cup. A reporter at the Mobile races noted in 1851 that when women were in the crowd, "not a squabble, dispute, or angry word, took place upon the course."[38] Some racing supporters, in fact, advocating attracting more women to the racecourse to help improve racing's tarnished reputation.[39] There is no evidence to suggest, however, that women took the lead in a movement against either gambling or the races in Baltimore, Norfolk, and Richmond. Although women were very influential, in this case their attitude was indistinguishable from that of other critics of games.

Clearly, the decline of public gambling was not simply a manifestation of a new aversion to gaming. Rather, it seems that the shifting

The Decline of Gambling and Horse Racing

attitudes were more closely related to the role gaming played in society. The function and, consequently, the value of public gambling underwent great changes during the first fifty years of the nineteenth century. When public gambling no longer served a symbolic and social function—when the upper class lost its central role in the gambling sphere—it gradually lost its popularity as an upper-class pastime and, consequently, its shield of legitimacy. Also, in most Southern communities new leadership began to replace the "old family" planter control. In developing urban centers like Baltimore, Norfolk, and Richmond, the planters who maintained city homes in addition to their plantation homes found themselves losing control to upcoming merchants, entrepreneurs, or industrialists, who found new ways to express their status.

In his study of poverty and social order in antebellum America, Raymond A. Mohl suggests that the social changes of this period were particularly disturbing to those who identified with the past. He notes that "for those who defined the public good in terms of self interest, disorder meant bad business and violence posed a very immediate personal danger."[40] Such irrational fears seem to have played a role in the upper class's response to public gambling and horse racing in Baltimore, Norfolk, and Richmond. Robert P. Sutton's study of the gentry in late Jeffersonian Virginia suggests that their loss of eminence on both the national and local levels led to suspicions that egalitarian sentiment would dismantle their ordered society. In 1830, for example, William Wirt predicted that the democratic trends would cause the Republic to "degenerate into a mob" that would rush into anarchy and then despotism.[41] The elite's fears of social disintegration may have heightened their awareness of public gambling's potential for instability at the very time that they were moving on to other, more private, gambling pursuits.

The manner in which the gambling laws were enforced says a great deal about their intent. Private gambling houses or clubs for the wealthy continued to operate, but the police were assiduous in arresting lower-class whites and blacks at public gambling houses. These groups, of course, were the people credited with creating social instability. Newspapers made much of the lower-class improprieties but rarely mentioned similar upper-class transgressions. Lower-class blacks and whites were arrested for attending and keeping "Negro Gambling Houses." Often the charges included "disturbing the peace of the neighborhood" or "desecrating the Sabbath"—reflecting the underlying fears of disorder. Police were especially alert to blacks gambling in homes, raiding these private dens with vengeance both before the Civil War and after.

The police were also wary of blacks or lower-class whites who possessed professional gambling equipment. The attention to blacks' gambling was equaled only by the concerns about "colored brothels." In fact, the two were frequently connected. When a Richmond free mulatto was brought before the mayor in 1853 for running an entertainment house for slaves, his guilt was compounded by the presence of prostitutes at his establishment. In addition to corrupting the slaves' morals by selling them liquor, the defendant was accused of allowing visits by "ladies (of a certain class) rustling in silks and as odoriferous as pinks or honeysuckle."[42]

The upper-class gambling houses or "gentlemen's clubs," meanwhile, were one area where the semblance of upper-class control was maintained. Magnificently appointed, these resorts were often small self-contained worlds that set the rich apart and, at the same time, hid their activities. The proprietor of the gaming house of Slater's, a Baltimore establishment popular in the 1860s, ordered his doorkeeper not to admit anyone unless he had been invited. He furnished, at no charge, liquors, afternoon dinner, and late-night suppers. An advertisement for Slater's replacement, the gaming house of Slater, Kirby, and Parker, suggests the atmosphere:

> The building in itself is an old one, and has long been used as a sporting establishment, but the proprietors becoming ambitious, and the "gentlemen" of Baltimore complaining of the want of a first-class "club house," it has undergone a complete renovation, the floors in the upper part of the building being raised four feet each. . . . The upper story is divided into private club-rooms, bed-chambers, bath-rooms, and wine-closets. A large cellar extends the length of the building underground, and a private entrance leads out into the open lot on a back street, through which the visitors can pass if desirous of shunning the main entrance.[43]

Obviously, some hypocrisy was involved here; the description brings to mind shadowy figures sneaking out a back door and stealthily boarding their waiting carriages. There are, however, deeper implications. This type of gambling house was an opulent second home for those who

The Decline of Gambling and Horse Racing

could afford it. Because only a small portion of the population could afford such luxury, the clientele was limited to the upper class. The upper class did not indicate a strong dislike for gambling itself but for gambling's potential for social disruption. Gambling inside the club house, cut off from general society, was not perceived as a threat to social order. Although the houses were often operated by professional gamblers, the upper-class patrons felt that the club was their domain. Apparently, they saw no contradiction in criticizing the disorder accompanying public gambling while simultaneously patronizing private gambling resorts themselves.

One of the most intriguing paradoxes of nineteenth-century gambling is the way the upper class helped to alter the general public perception of gambling while continuing to support its own gambling habits in private. Games of chance were associated with "low-life" or rowdies; clergy, outspoken citizens, and the press stigmatized patrons of public gambling dens. The transience induced by the Civil War, with its accompanying drinking, looting, and gambling, reinforced the image. One of the Richmond newspapers accused the large number of faro banks and bars of being the source of most wartime street problems in that city, which acquired a reputation for having numerous gambling resorts.[44] When stationed there, young H. A. Tutwiler, a soldier from Alabama, received a clipping from home describing the Richmond faro banks. In response, he indicated their extensiveness: "What did you mean by sending me that piece about the faro banks on Main Street? Did you think anyone could stay a month in this city without knowing that there were such places all over the city? Or did you write to inform me in case I did not know where they were."[45]

In addition to denouncing the degraded state of public gambling and the involvement of professional operators, upper-class citizens also removed themselves from public amusements that had obvious gambling connections, such as public horse races. As a result, the quality of the field declined, crowd size dwindled, and the spectators who did come were noticeably more boisterous than their counterparts from an earlier time. The more the upper class removed itself, the more the situation became a self-fulfilling prophecy. In the 1850s there were numerous reports of disorderly outbursts, particularly shootings, that stemmed from loud arguments over bets.[46] As Samuel Mordecai observed, the racetrack had degenerated into a haven for the rougher elements of society.

In Virginia the elite remained aloof from horse racing; there was no successful attempt to create state-controlled tracks or betting. The story in Maryland was different, because some of the elite took a different approach to the problem. As in Virginia, racing in postwar Maryland remained in a state of disrepute; no organized jockey club existed in Maryland at the close of the Civil War. Some of the leading citizens, however, were not willing to accept the situation, particularly because Maryland horses were still winning honors at Northern courses. George Washington Howard, a contemporary observer, reported that the winner of the Saratoga Cup at the 1868 Saratoga race meeting gave a dinner soon after his victory. Maryland's governor, Oden Bowie, was among the guests. This group, Howard observed, came up with the idea of creating a well-regulated track, "to be presided over by gentlemen and from which, fraud and rascality, so often in the past unpleasant concomitants of the course, should be banished." The result was the Maryland Jockey Club and the Pimlico Course on the outskirts of Baltimore.[47]

From the beginning, as Howard noted, it was clear that gentlemen were once again in control of the track. It is also significant that, reminiscent of the early nineteenth century, the gentry had its own distinct space—seats and boxes—at trackside. The difference in approaches taken in Maryland and Virginia, particularly the contrast between Baltimore and Richmond, more than likely had less to do with attitudes toward racing than the postwar economies of the two areas. Those who might have supported a new track in Richmond were busy rebuilding the city and their own fortunes.

Upper-class citizens in both states did, however, continue to develop their own exclusive horse games. For many, private clubs that featured steeplechasing, point-to-point matches, and fox hunts replaced the old jockey clubs and public racing. The gentry remained aloof from trotting events, a sport which became very popular among the middle class in the 1850s. The main thing that distinguished trotting from horse racing was cost. Those who could not afford to breed fine horses could own a trotting horse, hitch it to a roadster, and compete. Trotting, as horseman William Henry Herbert noted in 1857, was a sport of the people: "It is the trial-ground and arena for the roadster, open to every one who

The Decline of Gambling and Horse Racing

keeps a horse for his own driving . . . the butcher, the baker, or the farmer, who keeps his own fast crab, trains it himself into general condition on the road, and puts it for a month or two into the hands of Spicer, Woodruff, Wheelan, or some other tip-top-sawyer, to bring it to its best time, and trot it, when the purse is to be won."[48]

Trotting matches were frequently held in conjunction with agricultural fairs, prompting one critic to complain that trotting was replacing other, more educational events at such exhibitions. The agricultural fair, he noted, had degenerated into "a plow, a pumpkin, a pig, and two hundred and fifty trotting horses."[49] All three cities had trotting courses; both Norfolk and Richmond had trotting courses with connections to the fairgrounds. Competition among trotters was fierce. Consequently, betting between spectators was fairly common, although there is little indication that professional gamblers organized to take bets, presumably because the stakes were not very high. The upper class's reluctance to participate in such an innocuous sport indicates the extent to which public racing in general no longer served social functions for the elite. At the same time, it also mirrored the upper class's latent fear of the social instability inherent in unregulated public gatherings. The upper class's response to trotting was to insure that it was well-regulated and policed.

The trend during the nineteenth century was toward stricter regulation of public gaming amusements or amusements with gaming potential. Among the upper and middle classes there was a definite change in attitudes toward gaming sports, but the result was not simply an antigambling stance, particularly on the part of the upper class. Although they did not question their own private gambling, some upper-class citizens perceived that uncontrolled gambling among the masses could threaten the social order. The rate of gambling-related disturbances had not increased significantly since the early part of the century, but larger urban populations and the number of transients heightened the general awareness of the problem of rowdies, a problem that was magnified by the upper class's distance from those who were involved in public gambling. (In contrast, the upper class seemed less worried about rowdies in the theater, perhaps because many of the theater rowdies were drunken young aristocrats.) The immediate result was a complex system of laws ostensibly aimed at eradicating the gambling problem but actually intended to eliminate the professional gambler and to control the gambling that took place outside of the purview of the upper class. Gradually, also, the elite citizens of Baltimore, Norfolk, and Richmond severed their relationship with public gaming amusements, preferring instead to express their status in other ways.

Chapter Five

Self-Definition through Clubs and Organizations

In 1877 historian John H. Hewitt noted that "hardly any man rose to eminence for half a century in Baltimore who had not been a member of the Jefferson," the most prestigious debating society.[1] The Jefferson, like numerous other clubs and organizations, played an important role in the lives of those Baltimoreans who were lucky enough to be considered for membership. Throughout the nineteenth century, all sorts of citizens of Baltimore, Norfolk, and Richmond enjoyed memberships in a variety of clubs and organizations. Although many of the clubs were founded for serious purposes, participation provided amusement, and thus club work offers another window on nineteenth-century amusement habits. More than any other amusement, clubs allowed participants to distinguish themselves from others based upon interests, religion, ethnicity, and social status.[2]

Various library, literary, and debating societies flourished in upper-class circles, providing forums for the upper class—particularly upper-class men—to socialize and share ideas. The Library Society of Richmond supported a private reading room for its members' exclusive use. As John Hewitt observed, members of such clubs were also local leaders. For example, the Delphian Club, formed in Baltimore in the second decade of the nineteenth century, included many prominent men on its roster. Charter members included General William H. Winder, John Pierpoint, and J. H. B. Latrobe, while later rosters included John Pendleton Kennedy, Robert Goodloe Harper, Francis Scott Key, Rembrandt Peale, and William Wirt.[3]

Membership in the Delphian was intellectually rewarding, but it was also very fashionable. The word "fashionable" is encountered so frequently in upper-class descriptions of their own literary club activities that it is hard to escape the conclusion that this elusive attribute was the impetus for much upper-class participation. The element of instruction gave popular sanction to groups that were often really social, and sometimes frivolous, in nature. More important, such clubs provided the opportunity for social interaction. An important question, of course, is whether the leaders chose the clubs or the clubs made the leaders. Did the social, economic, and political leadership naturally seek out memberships in clubs with their peers? Or did membership in the clubs provide connections and access to power? The answer is complex, for clubs played a variety of roles in private and public life. In addition to social interaction, nineteenth-century clubs offered opportunities for expressing social status, for control and regulation of others, and for framing a new economic and social order.

Club roles from Baltimore, Norfolk, and Richmond indicate that until the 1820s clubs were still primarily upper-class in nature, although there were some middle-class charitable societies that were church-related. The upper-class character of club activity was a legacy from the eighteenth century, when the only people who had time or money for club participation were the landed gentry. Club membership distinguished the upper class, both by virtue of the activity involved and by the way the club members as a corporate body acted toward those below them. The sporting clubs that emulated British models—cricket clubs, for example—were obviously upper-class in membership.[4] Acceptance into membership meant social acceptance. The unspoken membership requirement was high social status. Similarly, the jockey clubs that were established to promote horse racing were upper-class in nature. The exclusiveness of jockey clubs, as well as the clubs' control of racing, grew out of a structured society and, in turn, helped to maintain that structure.

The early nineteenth-century benevolent societies were a complex mixture of the practical and the social, becoming even more socially oriented as the century progressed. Established in the late eighteenth and early nineteenth centuries as relief associations, Richmond's Female Humane Association and its male counterpart, the Amicable Society, were typical of upper-class charitable organizations in Baltimore, Norfolk, and Richmond. Members were social, political, and religious leaders of the city. Founders of the Female Humane Association included Mrs. James Wood (wife of the former governor) and Mrs. Philip N.

Nicholas (wife of the attorney general). This organization aided indigent women of the city and built a home for needy girls in 1811. While charitable in intent, the meetings of the Female Humane Association provided another source of social intercourse for upper-class women. Association work also provided a means for expressing social rank during a period when lines were not so strictly drawn in public amusements. The Amicable Society had a similar dual function. In every instance of providing relief to the poor and to strangers, the upper-class members subtly asserted their superior social position.[5]

Most members of the Amicable Society were also members of the Quoit Club (also known as the Barbeque Club), a social club composed of upper-class men who met at Buchanan Spring (north of the city) on alternate Saturdays from the first of May until October. The men played quoits, a game similar to horseshoes, and dined together. Members included judges, lawyers, doctors, selected ministers, and merchants, plus the governor of Virginia, who had a general invitation upon entering office. Members called regularly at the best hotels to see if distinguished travelers were registered; they then invited the visitors to the next Quoit Club meeting.[6] Thus, while social, the club bolstered the political network and reinforced the established leadership.

Beginning in the late 1820s middle-class citizens, especially women, got more involved in creating their own charitable and benevolent societies, especially organizations with religious connections—the Catholic Orphan Asylum, the Female Penitent's Refuge Society, the Impartial Humane Society, the Mary and Martha Society, the Dorcas Society, and many others that have disappeared without a trace. Most historians have noted that the increased enthusiasm for benevolent work was a product of religious revivals in the 1820s. Most likely that was the case in Baltimore, Norfolk, and Richmond as well, but contemporaries did not spend much time writing about the reasons for their increased charitable activities. The work of the Female Humane Association or the Amicable Society indicates, however, that an interest in benevolence on the part of both men and women preceded any revivals of the 1820s.

The greater middle-class involvement in clubs and benevolent organizations after the 1820s altered the value of upper-class memberships in such organizations. Although upper-class women continued to participate in charitable societies, increasingly during the nineteenth century the upper class turned to memberships in social clubs like the Quoit

Club to express superior social status. Meanwhile, middle-class membership in private organizations and societies continued to serve functions other than those for which the organizations were ostensibly founded. Middle-class women, as Suzanne Lebsock has aptly delineated, created a separate sphere in which they could assert themselves in positions of leadership and, perhaps more important, handle large sums of money. The thrust of both men's and women's charity work in Baltimore, Norfolk, and Richmond seems to have been to aid individuals, particularly orphans and poor women, rather than to reform society in general or control the poor. Nevertheless, one important consequence of middle-class club work was to set the middle-class members apart from and above the lower classes, while club activities also provided social outlets and opportunities for self-improvement. [7]

Some middle-class organizations were direct imitations of upper-class institutions. In Baltimore in 1839 the merchants' clerks founded the Mercantile Library Association, a circulating library that featured a reading room. Although it was open to "all classes of our citizens, ladies as well as gentlemen," the middle-class founders discouraged lower-class membership by requiring the payment of annual dues. This organization was clearly one that sought to stimulate the cultural development of its upwardly mobile members. Baltimore historian George W. Howard noted that only those books that were "likely to elevate the tone, or encourage the literary taste of the reader" were placed upon the shelves. [8]

Military organizations experienced a revival in the 1830s because of middle-class involvement. All three cities had numerous militia units; Richmond, for example, had at least eight. At a time when some people seemed to be concerned about the exuberant rowdiness growing out of political democracy, military companies such as the First Baltimore Invincibles, the Norfolk Light Artillery Blues, and the Richmond Light Infantry Blues epitomized order and patriotism. Each corps had its own organizational structure, as well as a distinctive uniform, which the members proudly wore when companies paraded in celebration of patriotic holidays or special events. Besides providing comradery and social opportunities, the military organizations earned members a certain amount of respect from the community at large. Holding an office in a company also accorded some members higher social status. [9]

Similarly, during the first decades of the century, the middle-class members of volunteer fire companies found fellowship and earned respect by virtue of their participation in such organizations. Again, they received popular recognition because of their service to the community and their public appearances in parades and other celebrations. Visitor Henry Murray noted that the people in Baltimore who enjoyed the widest reputation were the fire company volunteers. In Richmond the organizations formed a fire insurance company. Every volunteer was required to possess at least one share of stock to indicate his own interest "in preventing and putting out fires." [10]

Fire companies did, however, have a rowdy side. From their inception, they had attracted a crowd of followers who developed strong allegiances to particular engine companies. This often produced intense rivalries between companies, as well as races to fires. The custom of having supernumerary members, or runners, usually young boys, added to the rowdiness produced by the rivalries. Baltimore historian J. Thomas Scharf commented on the developing split in the engine company ranks, distinguishing between the lawless followers and the older middle-class members:

> Youth not controlled by parental restraint, as soon as the shades of night close in, sought the engine-houses, where hours were spent in the rehearsal of deeds of violence and crime, the planning of attacks on rival companies, or in scheming for the application of the incendiary match without danger of detection. . . . These riots were created and participated in by a certain class known as "hangers-on" and "runners." Many worthy citizens belonged to the companies, and exerted themselves to the utmost to prevent or check these evils. [11]

The extent to which the fire companies served a social function beyond mere fire prevention is evident in the rapidity with which the respectable middle-class citizens gave up membership when the lower-class rowdies began to fill the membership ranks and cause disturbances.

Although Norfolk did not suffer so much from engine company rowdies, both Baltimore and Richmond were plagued by numerous incidents. Henry Murray noted that he observed a fire company in Richmond trying out its engines and hoses, followed "by a squad of the unwashed." The rowdy group somehow managed to get the hose and turn it on a coach containing two older women. [12] In 1836 Baltimore's mayor, Samuel Smith, complained that fire companies encouraged youths and apprentices to "assemble and carouse at the engine houses, causing fires or giving false alarms for mere diversion."[13] Noting rivalries between different parts of town, the *Baltimore Sun* blamed "five or six dozen of flash fellows,—fancy rattlers—tie and jewelry, who drink liquor enough to make it necessary either to go to bed or do something to work off the excitement." On New Year's Eve 1838, rowdies threw a fire engine off a dock.[14] The fire company rowdies were so numerous in Baltimore in the 1850s that they could influence local elections. Middle-class citizens sought to compensate and worked to institute a more responsive system. They joined with upper-class citizens in Baltimore to force the establishment of a paid fire department in 1858. Likewise, an independent police force, separate from local government, was established in 1860.[15]

By the 1840s most benevolent and fraternal organizations in Baltimore, Norfolk, and Richmond were middle-class in composition. The benevolent societies continued to aim most of their efforts at bettering the conditions of the poor. Middle-class respectability was enhanced while the social distance between the lower and middle classes widened. Middle-class fraternal orders such as the Druids, the Odd Fellows, the Tribe of Red Men, and the Masons did many beneficial things for their communities. Their primary effect, however, was to distinguish the respectable middle-class citizens from the middle class in general and the lower class. The systems of interclub benevolence, especially the care of members' families, insured that members would not lapse into poverty. At the same time, the membership dues and the secret membership selection process kept most lower-class citizens out of these societies and helped form linkages that were important outside of club work.[16]

The temperance organizations that flourished in Baltimore, Norfolk, and Richmond in the 1830s and 1840s were benevolent and fraternal. They were also social, providing purposeful amusement. Because many of the changes in form and function that these temperance organizations displayed during the period before the Civil War reflect changes in the general function of associations during this period, they are an especially good example of middle-class organizations. The first Virginia temperance organization was formed in 1826 at Ash Camp Meeting-house in Charlotte County by eleven men, mostly clergy. From this inauspicious start, the societies grew rapidly; there were more than fifty in 1829 and two hundred and fifty by 1836. Estimates of membership varied, but it

Self-Definition through Organizations

was well over 50,000 by 1836 in Virginia alone. Richmond's societies had over 1,000 members in 1834. There were even special societies for youth. On May Day in 1848, Norfolk hosted a Grand Juvenile Temperance Celebration. [17]

Although there were a few temperance societies for blacks in Richmond and Baltimore, there is no evidence that common laborers or poor whites were involved until mid-century. Most of the upper class also stood aloof from membership. An article in the *Virginia Historical Register* in 1850 noted that only one or two nonclerical members of the upper class failed to go along with the belief of their peers that temperance reform was impossible. In their study of Virginia liquor legislation, C. C. Pearson and J. Edwin Hendricks note that the upper class's response to the drinking problem was half-hearted and paternalistic. Doubting the possibility of temperance reform, upper-class citizens supported the passage of laws to punish excessive drinking in public rather than control consumption in general. [18] The upper class was more interested in controlling rowdy outbursts than improving the wretched lives of habitual drunkards.

Thus, temperance in Baltimore, Norfolk, and Richmond was predominantly a middle-class movement, and until the 1840s it was predominantly male. Temperance reformer Lucian Minor noted: "The middle classes, always apt to be foremost in useful virtues, were the main adherents of the Temperance Reformation. The two extremes of society—the very lowest, and those who (especially in their own estimation) stood highest, agreed in disdaining the movement." Minor attributed the middle-class interest to the contacts that the middle class had with the lower class. Middle-class Baptists and Methodists, he concluded, were "nearer to the lower classes." They often did mission work in "haunts of squalid wretchedness" and saw firsthand the "scenes of filthy, ragged vice." [19] Just as in the gambling legislation, the evangelical thrust in Maryland and Virginia aimed to reform individuals rather than society in general. Similarly, temperance was a movement by and for individuals.

Although the middle-class awareness (and perhaps fear) of drunkenness stimulated an interest in temperance, it did not initially cause these middle-class organizations to invite drunkards—or the lower class in general—to membership in the temperance societies. They sponsored public addresses and circulated tracts and books among the poor but maintained a distinction between members and nonmembers. The early temperance societies solicited middle-class men for membership. The Fourth Report, 1831, of the American Temperance Society made this point very forcefully: "Temperance Societies are designed for temperate men. Their object is to keep all sober who are so now; till all the drunkards, who will not reform, are dead, and the world is free."[20] Assessing the effects of the temperance societies, one of the movement's founders, Jeremiah Jeter, noted that the impact on the middle class had been extensive: "It will hardly be denied, by candid and observant men, that the Temperance Society has accomplished great good: light has been extensively diffused; the habits of society, especially of the middle classes, have been manifestly improved; the quantity of ardent spirit consumed has been much diminished."[21]

Temperance societies were similar to middle-class clubs in the way they served a dual function. Besides promoting opportunities for fellowship, membership brought respectability and social status and distinguished members from the drunkards who could not or would not improve themselves. Middle-class members sought to improve their own social status by altering the definition of gentleman. The real gentleman was moderate, sober, and stable, in contrast to the immoral profligacy of the upper class and the overindulgence of some of the lower class. The new definition was particularly important for the upwardly mobile middle class.

In 1840 an event occurred that nearly split the temperance cause in two. The Washingtonians, a temperance organization that solicited members from the intemperate, was founded in Baltimore. The Washingtonians preached the possibility of reform of all drunkards and, consequently, drew members from the lower and middle classes. In contrast to the older temperance organizations, the Washingtonians urged total abstinence. Three of the original members, J. G. Pollard, W. E. Wright, and Christian Keener, toured the major cities of Virginia and were successful in convincing many to take the abstinence pledge. In Richmond, for example, it was estimated that 800 or 900 took the pledge. South of Richmond, in Petersburg, 1,000, including 300 blacks, took the pledge.[22]

The Washingtonians aroused interest through parades, picnics, dinners, and celebrations of public holidays—all without the accompaniment of intoxicating spirits. In Baltimore the Washingtonians did not schedule outside speakers. Rather, they held "experience meetings" where the reformed could tell stories of their degeneration and later redemption by temperance. Older temperance leaders resented the new societies' methods as well as their principles. In particular, the middle-class leadership of the older societies did not approve of the more open membership of the Washington societies; once the reform effort was opened to everyone, the middle-class reformers lost some of their social leverage.[23]

At the same time, the creation of the Washingtonians and its sister organization, the Martha Washingtonians, indicates the extent to which some of the lower class had developed an appreciation for self-improvement. The Martha Washingtonians were generally laborers—women who did not possess much in the way of earthly comforts. Yet, as contemporary historian Lorenzo Dow Johnson noted in 1843, these women joined together to use what resources they possessed to provide relief for others. Johnson underscored that the ladies "who have but little or nothing themselves to give, associate together in societies, where they can turn to some good account, a little portion of *time* or the service of their hands, either in working, or visiting the poor." The work of the Martha Washingtonians indicated "that *all*, all classes of human beings, irrespective entirely of what they individually possess, may share in the luxury of doing good." Johnson credited the Martha Washingtonians with the decrease in the incidence of intoxication in Baltimore, noting that in 1842 more than forty children who were living in the Orphan Asylum were returned to reformed, sober parents.[24]

Historians of some of the industrialized cities of the Northeast emphasize the role that working people played in reform efforts but note that differences in cultural background led to divisions over the issue of temperance. Jill Siegel Dodd's study of antebellum Boston, for example, underscores that some workingmen "wholeheartedly embraced the new way of life . . . and actively encouraged their fellow workingmen to do the same," while others "clung fiercely to their customary way of life." Dodd notes that it is difficult to determine whether temperance caused upward mobility or "whether being socially mobile encouraged the adoption of a complex of behavior patterns, among them temperance."[25]

Of the three cities in this study, ironically, resistance to temperance was strongest in Baltimore, home of the Washingtonians. Most of the opposition came from the large German community, particularly from the Turners, an organization that opposed the imposition of morals by Catholics and Methodists.[26] Although working people did not uniformly embrace temperance organizations in Norfolk and Richmond, there was little overt resistance to temperance efforts there, perhaps because the immigrant communities were smaller. The enthusiastic efforts of those working people who were involved in temperance societies suggest that they were well aware of the self-improvement aspect; some saw temperance as the key to upward mobility.

Temperance societies took yet another turn with the founding of a temperance-related fraternal order, the Sons of Temperance. The first Sons of Temperance organization in Virginia was established in Norfolk in 1843. Despite objections to its secrecy and fears that it was politically subversive, the Sons spread rapidly. In 1852 the Richmond City Directory listed eleven divisions, and women had their own Sisters of Temperance. Members were mostly middle or lower-middle class, including many ministers, doctors, small merchants, farmers, teachers, and lawyers.[27] While the Sons required a total abstinence pledge, one of the other purposes of the organization was to provide a place for members to spend leisure time, as two of the organization's leaders noted in 1848: "Our halls are also intended to be pleasant places of resort of social intercourse, in which young men especially may acquire habits of public speaking, and of transacting the business of a popular assembly; and by which many who have leisure, may be lured from the bar-room and other scenes of dissipation."[28] The Sons recognized the growing distinction between work and leisure and attempted to fill leisure with constructive activities that encouraged self-improvement. Thus, members would have an edge over nonmembers in the social mobility game.

Like other fraternal orders, the Sons also provided aid to members and their families. Most of the society's benevolent efforts were, in fact, limited to the membership of the fraternity. Although the society attempted to win converts to the idea of total abstinence among the lower class, there were limits when it came to election to membership. The Sons rejected anyone who could not earn his own livelihood or who had no means of support. A comparable organization, the Independent Order of Rechabites, required that a prospective member be free from "all bodily disease or infirmity that would render him burdensome to the tent."[29] These lower- and middle-class temperance organizations drew a distinction between the worthy, self-improvement conscious segment of the lower class and those who were more or less permanently mired at the bottom. The status of members was reinforced by underscoring the distance between them and those below them.

By 1860 charitable and benevolent organizations could be found throughout the population, white and black. Free blacks in antebellum Baltimore were particularly active in creating such clubs, as well as a variety of secret societies. In Baltimore, for example, the Sisters of Providence, a society of black women, was very active and established a school for black girls in 1829. Baltimore free blacks also sponsored lyceums for self-improvement. Although evidence of slave organizations is less apparent, John O'Brien has concluded that the involvement of Richmond slaves in clandestine societies and church work prepared them for leadership in the postwar period. Freedmen themselves noted in a meeting at Richmond's First African Church in December 1865 that for twenty-five or thirty years they had had societies with "the benevolent object of caring for the sick, aged and infirm, and of securing the rights of a decent and Christian burial for our dead." Richmond free blacks formed the African Burial Society in 1815 and the Union Burial Ground Society in 1847. Whenever possible, free blacks also organized to preserve rights. In Norfolk, for example, the Colored Monitor Union Club was formed on April 4, 1865, to promote equality and suffrage. Moreover, after the war, blacks were quick to organize military companies in all three cities; members wore uniforms, met for nightly drills, and participated in parades. While whites often felt threatened by the black units, the black community accorded members special prestige.[30]

In Richmond, Jews had been welcomed into social clubs such as the Amicable Society from their inception; there was much social intermingling during the early part of the century. After the big influx of Jewish immigration in the 1830s, there was less mixing, most likely because there was more of a Jewish community. Similarly, there was little social mingling in Baltimore, where there were distinctive Jewish neighborhoods.[31] By the 1840s Jews and Germans in both cities had created their own clubs and organizations. These were not totally emulative of the elite organizations, for the immigrants brought organizational models with them from Europe. Nevertheless, in style and approach the immigrant club members took many of their ideas from what they saw in the American clubs.

Immigrant benevolent organizations provided charity for indigent immigrants, social opportunities, and education in American ways. All of this was especially important in Baltimore, which had large populations of immigrant Germans, Irish, and Jews. As Kathy Peiss notes, participation in American clubs afforded immigrants a new conception of leisure—"the idea of segmenting and organizing leisure into a distinct sphere of activity."[32] Club work also increased the respectability of the organizations and their members, distinguishing them from other, "lower-class," immigrants who did not actively set out to help themselves. Jewish citizens formed B'nai B'riths and Young Men's Hebrew Associations, both primarily educational and recreational. Baltimore's Jewish Harmony Circle provided its members with a reading room, a ladies' parlor, and a billiard room; sponsored dances; and worked for charitable causes.[33] Baltimore's German immigrants formed various singing societies, such as the Liederkranz and the Germania Mannechor, as well as fraternal orders such as the Schiller Grove of Druids, the Red Men's Saengerbund, the Osceola tribe of German Red Men, and various gymnastic clubs. Baltimore's working-class Germans also founded the German Workingmen's Relief Association and the Schützengesellschaft (shooting club), which operated Schuetzen Park, a recreation area that included picnic areas, target ranges, bowling alleys, and dance floors in the mid 1800s.[34]

In 1865 the *Baltimore American* noted that "the numbers, wealth, and importance of our German fellow citizens have increased to such proportions that their institutions and influences are sensibly felt by the community at large."[35] The older, more established German immigrants formed a number of clubs that were active in civic work. The most exclusive was the Germania Club (founded in 1840). Next was Concordia (formed in 1847), which emphasized literary and musical programs appealing to the upper middle class. Members of both the Germania and the Concordia were mostly wealthy merchants, with familial and social ties to Bremen. One significant consequence of club membership for these merchants was the creation of valuable social and trade networks; the merchants took tobacco to Bremen and brought German immigrants to Baltimore. Later, when German Jewish citizens began to play a significant role in the Concordia Club, the non-Jewish German citizens dropped out and the club became almost exclusively Jewish.[36]

Self-Definition through Organizations

As the number of clubs increased in the nineteenth century, and just about anyone could be a member of some organization, the upper class responded by turning to exclusive social clubs. There was not even the pretense of instruction or benevolence; there were, however, stringent controls over membership and assessment of high dues, distinguishing the upper class as a group that had both the time and the money to participate in such activity. Significantly, the Civil War did not greatly alter upper-class club participation or the trend toward clubs that were purely social. During the war private parties and clubs provided much of the available entertainment when many of the public sources were limited. Richmond's Starvation Club, a group of young people who met weekly or semiweekly to present plays, dances, or other amusements, grew out of the war conditions. The club took its name from the absence of refreshments when the blockade made obtaining party food impossible. At the same time, those who attended the parties were self-consciously aware of the patriotic nature of their gesture. Their "deprivation" bound them together and made them more conscious of their elite social position.[37] After the war, when fortunes were lost and the old upper class was struggling to reassert itself, clubs provided an important means of declaring status.

The Allston Association, which had evolved from a group of "gentlemen and artists" who met to discuss art, music, and literary events to a group that came together merely for games and recreation, was one of the more elite clubs in Baltimore. Perhaps even more exclusive was the Maryland Club, chartered in 1858 specifically to promote social relations among its members. Membership was considered "just about the highest social honor to which a male Baltimorean [could] aspire."[38]

Richmond's Home Club was typical of these upper-class organizations. Popular in the 1840s, the club met in private homes, with no purpose other than amusement. Membership was by election and was limited to thirty persons; one blackball could exclude a person. Some topics of conversation were not allowed, to assure that talk was not too serious. In 1851 John P. Little noted that a similar organization, the Owl Club, was composed of "wits and fun lovers." The purpose was openly social. Richmond's Arlington Social and Pleasure Club likewise made no pretense of being anything other than an amusement-oriented group. The Richmond Club, and later the Westmoreland Club, attracted members because of the element of exclusion. As late as 1888 a duel between Dr. George Ben Johnston and John S. Wise was narrowly averted after Wise discovered that his nomination for membership in the Westmoreland Club had been blackballed.[39]

Norfolk's upper class also began to form exclusive social clubs in the 1840s. Again, the aspect of benevolence or charity was played down, and the members were cliquish in their restrictive membership policies. The Norfolk German Club, formed in 1868, combined many of the elements of these earlier elite organizations. This particular club was organized to sponsor private dances that featured the patterned German dance that was very popular in the postwar period. It originally consisted of twelve couples who took turns holding the dances in their double parlors. There was a bit of reverse snobbery, for it was customary for the names of the participants not to be printed in the local newspapers. Contemporaries testify that even when the club grew larger, the members continued to be "the elite, beauty and fashion" of Norfolk.[40]

In the harbor cities of Baltimore and Norfolk, boat races had been popular since the early part of the century. They were similar to the horse races in that they were organized and controlled by the upper class, although anyone could be a spectator. In the postwar period boating became a club sport, and thus more exclusive. Besides distinguishing the members, such clubs provided training in leadership. Meetings provided opportunities for social intercourse between members of individual clubs and between clubs. The upper-class sporting clubs bound the upper class together, much like the fraternal organizations provided cohesion for the middle class. Through these sporting clubs, upper-class values were practiced and learned in a social setting. The Ocean Pleasure Club founded in Norfolk in the 1870s owned a clubhouse on the water at Ocean View where members met for "pleasant recreation and social intercourse."[41]

As Stephen Hardy's study of sports clubs in nineteenth-century Boston indicates, such clubs offered a source of group identity and solidarity, as well as a means of assessing another person's social status in the impersonal urban environment. Sporting clubs "were a rapprochement with its [the city's] new order."[42] Benjamin G. Rader concludes that participation in appropriate sports marked a person's membership in the upper status group, but it "did not threaten any deeply held personal

Self-Definition through Organizations

beliefs that might otherwise divide members of the elite." Rader also notes that younger men used membership in athletic clubs as a stepping stone to membership in exclusive men's clubs.[43]

Obviously, many factors played a part in the change in upper-class club orientation from the practical with social overtones to the purely social. One factor, of course, was the growing acceptance of entertainment. By the last half of the nineteenth century, clubs did not have to have a benevolent or educational justification. Another factor was the upper class's desire to separate themselves socially from the rising middle class. When middle-class citizens appropriated upper-class amusements, the upper class moved on to new forms. While the middle class attempted to achieve respectability through membership in benevolent or charitable organizations, the upper class sought to maintain social distance by creating clubs that had no practical purpose—clubs that existed solely for members' pleasure. Obviously, these exclusive clubs also provided opportunities for the upper class to express social status and to interact with their peers.

Clubs and organizations provided many services in developing urban areas. Benevolence, fire protection, police protection, cultural events, and an emphasis on sobriety were just a few of the contributions that such groups made in nineteenth-century Baltimore, Norfolk, and Richmond. Just as significant, however, were the contributions that were more subtle—things related to community but more specifically related to how people organized themselves with respect to one another. Participation in clubs provided a simple method of self-definition. At times this was divisive, as fire company rivalries suggest. Nevertheless, overall the separation into various clubs served less to create dissension than to create an order based on linkages forged in club work. The irony is that club membership, one of the most open expressions of democracy, helped to erect and maintain a social order based on a fairly rigid social stratification.

Chapter Six

··

Resorts of Amusement
and Status

·· In 1807 British visitor Charles William Janson commented on the social
mixing in taverns in the Upper South, noting rather disdainfully that
there was "generally no other accommodation than a large sitting-room,
in common, where the governor of the state, and the judge of this
district, in travelling, must associate with their fellow-citizens of every
degree."[1] During the early part of the century, public resorts did not
reflect social stratification, in part because there were so few public
amusement choices. Also, to be financially successful, a proprietor attempted to attract as many patrons as possible and excluded only the
known public nuisances. The owner of Richmond's City Tavern made
this clear in 1807 when he advertised his intention to pay "respected
attention . . . to *all* who may favor him with their custom."[2] Serving as
the commercial, social, and civic centers in an area, early nineteenth-
century taverns and inns were recognized as bastions of equality.

Similarly, the general public mixed freely at pleasure gardens, which
were family-oriented amusement centers in the early nineteenth century.
Serving ice cream and cake with various beverages, these establishments
often provided live entertainment—equestrians, ropedancers, musi-
cians—as well as games.[3] Coffeehouses were also frequented by all
classes. Baltimore historian J. Thomas Scharf observed that these places,
which sold light refreshments and subscribed to newspapers from various
parts of the country, supplied a common "clubhouse and an assembly-
room" to the citizens of the city.[4]

In his study of the early American inn, Paton Yoder notes that patrons
"did not really enjoy its democratic atmosphere, but, since there was no
alternative, they sometimes pretended and declared that they were
delighted in it." When choices did permit social distinctions, Yoder

concludes, the talk of equality was quickly abandoned.[5] This was true in Baltimore, Norfolk, and Richmond. Just as had happened with theater patronage, as more alternatives to the existing gardens and taverns opened, people sought to be with their peers; consequently, crowds in most amusement places became less heterogeneous.

Richmond's Eagle Tavern, for example, earned a reputation for serving prominent patrons, particularly because many members of the Virginia General Assembly lodged there. By 1817 the owner of Richmond's Spring Hill Gardens was advertising that he would not admit "Rough characters." In 1819 the proprietor of Norfolk's Delightful Retreat made a point of noting that he wished to provide a resort for "genteel residents and visitors of the Borough," both "Ladies and Gentlemen." The emphasis on genteel society was replicated in numerous advertisements, such as the one for the Public Garden on Briggs' Point in Norfolk in 1827. The owner noted that the resort was open "to the most genteel society" who could be assured "that the greatest good order and decorum will, at all times prevail there." Other taverns became hangouts for the lower class, especially newly arrived immigrants, such as the Irish and Germans. By mid-century in Baltimore, and to a lesser extent in Richmond, some Germans and Irish owned taverns that catered specifically to German or Irish immigrants.[6] Also by mid-century, taverns in general had been tainted by their association with gambling and gaming sports.

What is not clear is why certain establishments became resorts of the elite, when comparable places were not. Perhaps it had something to do with location or with the proprietor's pretensions. There is also not enough evidence to determine if initially the upper class's desire to separate was unique. The creation of clubs and organizations by the middle class and the establishment of taverns by immigrants suggest that the desire to associate with peers was probably generalized throughout the population. It aided in self-definition. What does seem to be unique to the upper class was a desire to use amusement choice to stay on top of the social hierarchy.

All this separation occurred, of course, while there was more talk of democracy. The tension between democratic ideals and hierarchical yearnings that shaped amusements and amusement habits in the nineteenth century usually led to a variety of types of the same amusement, with different participants—numerous theaters or clubs, for example. In addition, some amusements—such as exclusive horse games—were almost entirely the province of the elite. This was especially true of those amusements that required fairly large expenditures of money or, perhaps more important, time.

Informal visiting with neighbors, friends, or relatives often commanded large hunks of time. A carryover from the eighteenth century, visiting in the nineteenth century was distinguished by its extensiveness. The practice was common among all classes; travelers noted that even the slaves spent much of their free time visiting within their own cabins and at neighbors' cabins. Often, too, the visiting cut across age and sex barriers, because the family went together to call on friends and relatives. The busiest time for visiting, known as the "gay season," commenced with the Christmas holidays and lasted until mid-February.[7]

Visiting at parties was especially productive for the elite, who benefited from informal social contacts and introduced their sons and daughters to their social peers. Here children acquired a sense of being part of a special group or class, initiating contacts and friendships that lasted into adulthood. Young boys and girls were schooled in the social graces necessary to function at these entertainments. Dancing schools, for example, taught the latest steps, as well as other social amenities.[8]

In a series of letters to her mother, Ellen Wayles Randolph vividly described her activities as a young participant in the bustling elite party season of 1814 in Richmond. By March she was tiring of having to dress for visitors and complained that her Aunt Randolph would not let her rest, instead hurrying her out "to be introduced to a number of people." She wrote of attending a large party where "the company was gay and brilliant." Finally, in April she related her weariness "of the dissipated life" she was leading. She complained that she had no time for reading or writing—that her time was "divided between the business of dressing & the care of entertaining company."[9] Despite her youthful objections, however, the rounds of parties continued. Thomas Massie of Richmond wryly commented that even the influenza epidemic did not halt the partying or attempts at matchmaking in 1826. He noted that "the girls who were well enough" were still out looking for husbands and "would look for them in a grave yard if it were possible to find them there." One wonders what Massie would have said had he received an invitation to a funeral—a common practice among Richmond's elite by mid-century.[10]

In addition to the parties and dances, upper-class Baltimoreans threw lavish outdoor "Strawberry Parties" in the summer months. Again, one

Resorts of Amusement and Status

of the purposes was to give the young men and women opportunities to become better acquainted with others of their same social station. Such parties drew upper-class citizens together, while the excessive consumption distinguished them from other citizens. Servants offered strawberries and cream, pineapples, and champagne while an orchestra played quadrilles and waltzes. After dark, the festivities continued, usually inside the host's house.[11]

As the century progressed, the upper-class parties were increasingly distinguished from other parties by their ostentatious refreshment and entertainment. Even during the Civil War, contemporary reports noted the reckless expenditure of money. In 1864 the *Richmond Enquirer* complained, "Five balls advertised, and flour 125 dollars per barrel! . . . Who prates of famine and want?" Although the upper-class women of Richmond were involved in the war effort through their volunteer work at the hospitals and often were forced to make sacrifices, they also managed to give elegant luncheon and dinner parties. Mary Boykin Chesnut, for example, noted that despite the hardships, she still went to many luncheons. One that she attended in 1864 featured "Gumbo, ducks and olives, chickens in jelly, oysters, lettuce salad, chocolate cream, jelly cake, claret, champagne, etc."[12]

Confederate president Jefferson Davis and his wife gave bimonthly "levees" in Richmond for friends in government and military circles. These parties drew "a great many persons of high social position" and "the great, the noble, the *fair* of our land," according to contemporary assessments. These accounts also indicate that the guests were aware of their social status and quite proud of their attendance at such events. They spoke of meeting "all the elite of Richmond" or of enjoying the society of the ruling class. Another noted, "We should not expect suppers in these times, but we do have them! Champagne is $350 a dozen, but we sometimes have champagne! The confectioners charge $15 for a cake, but we have cake."[13]

In their continuous quest for distinction, the upper class found one amusement that maintained its exclusive nature throughout the century—spending summers at the western springs of Virginia or the eastern ocean resorts. To visit resorts at the springs or the beach, a person had to be wealthy enough to afford the trip and lodging, as well as the clothing and necessary gear. More than this, however, the person had to have a great amount of time free from work. In a period when time was increasingly measured in monetary terms, summering at resorts separated the elite from the pretenders on the basis of both money and time. It also brought them together with the elite from a variety of places. It was not uncommon for upper-class citizens from Baltimore, Norfolk, and Richmond to be together at the same resort.

When the springs first opened, they served a clientele of upper-class invalids who were joined by those interested in avoiding the unhealthy summer conditions in the cities, especially the oppressive heat. Advertisements noted the benefits of the water as an aid to the "prevention of disease or restoration of health." In 1811 Bowyer's White Sulphur Springs was advertised as a "FOUNTAIN OF HEALTH!" Advertisements for the Hygeia Hotel on the Chesapeake Bay at Old Point Comfort noted that "the salubrity of the climate," the "sea breezes," and "the hard sandy beach for Salt Water Bathing" made the area "the most desirable situation, perhaps, in the United States, for invalids." Visitors wrote of returning from Old Point "much improved in . . . health." As late as 1823 an advertisement for York Springs noted that the water benefited "bilious habits, jaundice, dyspepsia, rheumatism, gravel, tetter, &c." Some springs listed the results of chemical analysis of the water or offered the names of physicians who affirmed the medicinal powers of the water. [14]

Because of the number of sick people among the patrons, the springs were pretty dull in the early years of the century, as James Paulding noted in 1817: "Indeed the greater proportion of the company consists of invalids; and, of course, little amusement or gayety is to be found at these places. Bathing, drinking the waters, eating, and sleeping, are the principal occupations; and for recreation, they sometimes dance of evenings—when there is any music." [15] As the century progressed, people began to value resorts more for their social value than their medicinal benefits. The transition from health to entertainment, documented by contemporary advertisers and observations, occurred in the late 1810s and early 1820s. In 1813, for example, an advertisement for Bath Berkeley Springs praised the waters and also elaborately described the entertainment facilities. The latter included "a drawing room furnished for the Ladies, a Piano Forte, Maps of different kinds, Reading Room, &c.—a grand *Band of Music* for Balls, once or twice a week, as the company may think proper." [16] Other proprietors were more cautious. The owner of Shocco Springs in North Carolina advertised enter-

Resorts of Amusement and Status

tainment within the health setting. He noted that in addition to the "valuable Medicinal qualities," his resort was "surrounded by a polished society, where the invalid can be restored to health in an agreeable circle." The owner of Bedford Springs advertised that his resort would "gratify those who visit it for pleasure or health." In 1823 the Hygeia Hotel claimed to be "for invalids, as well as for those whose object is pleasure & amusement."[17]

By 1830 it was common to see advertisement headings that referred specifically to the "Public Entertainment" available at a particular spring. After his visit to the springs in the 1840s, George William Featherstonhaugh recorded that they were not popular "on account of their curative qualities, but because they are resorted to by the families of many opulent planters south and west of the Potomac."[18] Advertisements for Old Point Comfort in the 1840s described it as a retreat; there was no mention of sickness. When a correspondent to the *Richmond Enquirer* described his stay there in 1845, he emphasized the upper-class nature of the crowd and the amusements: "We left about 150 at the Point, and a gayer and happier set we never saw. What with music, dancing, ten-pins, billiards, sailing, fishing, and forming picturesque *tableaux-vivans* for the reflective power of Mr. Van Loan's Daguerrotype the moments flew by most rapidly." The transformation was complete by the last quarter of the century, when the springs were advertised under the column heading "Summer Resorts."[19]

The increased emphasis on entertainment at the resorts was typical of the general trend in the nineteenth century. As usual, the upper class was in the vanguard in its willingness to accept entertainment for its own sake. With the springs, also, the ability to go to such extremes for amusement set the upper class apart from the rest of society. Numerous historians have noted that one consequence of industrialization and factory work was the increasing distinction between work time and leisure time. It is ironic but understandable that upper-class citizens were among the first to proclaim their need for vacations and that they flaunted their status by participating in amusements requiring amounts of time or money not available to average citizens, much less factory workers. Certainly, some who most needed recreation at resorts could not afford it. For example, in the summer of 1857, Baltimorean John W. M. Williams confided to his diary that although he was "wonderfully prostrated in body & mind" by his work and his "family needed recreation also," it was too expensive to "take all to Cape May or any other watering place."[20]

One cannot help being struck by the upper class's constant awareness of the social value of what they were doing. Visitors at the springs wrote of being surrounded by "fashionable loungers" or "gay" crowds. Frequently, their letters described the arrival of others. Newspaper articles chronicled the presence of dignitaries or local gentry and suggest a sense of cliquishness. Typical of this genre, an article in the *Baltimore American* in August 1843 noted that President Tyler was expected at the White Sulphur Springs. It continued: "The South has already but a part of its contingent of wealth and fashion, and our own city is very fairly represented."[21]

Some of the resort patrons indicated that merely being part of the "fashionable crowd" was their primary reason for visiting the springs. People came, as one contemporary noted, "to see and be seen." An early historian of the springs noted that there was a "social taste" to the water—that the springs featured "a general muster under the banner of folly."[22] In 1851 a visitor to Nags Head, North Carolina, a beach resort that was popular with some of Norfolk's upper class, labeled it "the great hygeian resort of fashion and the graces." In 1860 a visitor to Nags Head observed that "fashion and frolic hold revel as though that remorseless leveler, old ocean, did not daily threaten a revolution." He also noted that the two to three hundred guests included "a full share of female loveliness."[23] Although the resort season ran from June through October, the "most fashionable period," as one patron of the springs noted, was from the middle of July until mid-September. "Gaity" was "at its height" during the month of August.[24]

Some resorts were considered more fashionable than others, and such assessments changed from year to year. In 1829 a writer in the *Baltimore American* commented on the unpredictable nature of the springs' reputations, as well as their exclusive patronage: "Fashion, ever wayward and capricious, and on no subject more so than the choice of a watering place to which she may summon her votaries, would seem by certain unequivocal indications to have selected the York Springs as her chosen place of resort at the approaching season of fashionable emigration . . . a name to which it was well entitled from its proximate geographical situation to our own city, and from its being the chosen resort of the leaders of the haut ton."[25]

Resorts of Amusement and Status

One of the constants in most letters from the resorts was the complaint of boredom, coupled with the idea that nonproductive idleness was a symbol of wealth. Some wrote of having to "kill time" or of being "busy doing nothing." Richmonder Littleton Wickham's description of life at the springs is typical and gives the sense of belonging to a special class: "Pardon me for not having written to you before now but you know the idle busy do nothing creative at the Springs with some trifle or other to occupy our attention now walking now visiting now bathing a routine of luxurious idleness which employs our time and yet gives us little or nothing to record."[26] One young woman thought that the idleness led to an unhealthy emphasis on "eating, drinking, and dressing." She disapprovingly reported that the "people seem to be given up to the gratification of every sin," making the springs "like Sodom and Gomorrah was, when it was destroyed with fire and brimstone."[27]

The emphasis on appearances led to ostentatious dress and dinners as guests at the resorts attempted to outshine one another. Doting fathers indulgently displayed their daughters in order to show off their wealth and, in turn, to attract wealthy sons-in-law. There was even competition in home building at the springs. As early as 1837 the *Richmond Enquirer* condemned this practice, noting that "the rich are beginning to vie with each other in these summer establishments."[28]

British visitors were often amazed that the upper class would be willing to crowd together in the resorts just for the sake of the social value. In 1835 Philip Nicklin visited the springs and observed that patrons were "willing to be crushed to death, to obtain a chance of laying their offerings on the shrine that fashion has set."[29] The exclusive nature of what went on at the springs also surprised many travelers who had thought Americans were more democratic. Captain Frederick Marryat commented on the "social taste" of the waters at the springs, particularly White Sulphur Springs. "It is at this place," he wrote, "that you feel how excessively aristocratical and exclusive the Americans would be, and indeed will be, in spite of their institutions."[30] Visitors noted that in addition to being from a prominent family, traveling by private carriage was frequently a requirement for accommodation at the springs.

Although there was much concern about the fate of the springs during the Civil War, the anxiety proved unwarranted. The springs continued to advertise, and at times conditions there were crowded. After the war, the seasons rapidly returned to normal, and resort owners remodeled old facilities and built some new ones. The *Norfolk Journal* reported in August 1867 that Nags Head had "never been patronized more than during the past season."[31]

In 1869 a Virginia Reconstruction Committee composed of former Confederate officers met at White Sulphur Springs. The photographs marking that occasion show them, as well as their wives and families. They had lost the war, but they had not lost their sense of style. To a great extent they symbolize all of the upper-class resort patrons. Despite the difficulties of wartime, especially the financial setbacks, the elite maintained appearances at the springs. Summering at resorts had become part of the upper class's way of life—an extravagant expression of an opulent life-style that marked their position in society. If anything, such expression was needed more after the war than before, as the elite, particularly Richmond's elite, sought to put their lives and fortunes in order and to recover their former positions.[32]

Trips to the springs obviously were out of the question for the common laborer. In part, stratification in a particular amusement—separate seating, for example—and of the kinds of amusements—the upper-class clientele of the springs versus the middle-class clientele of exhibitions, for example—was a consequence of ticket prices. Table 2 indicates the average cost of some popular public amusements in the

Table 2. Average price of an adult amusement ticket in Baltimore, Norfolk, and Richmond, 1810–70

	1810	1820	1830	1840	1850	1860	1870
Circus (box seat)	$1.00	.75	.50	.50	.50	—	—
Circus (gallery)	.75	.50	.25	.25	.25	—	—
Excursions	—	—	—	—	.50	1.00	—
Exhibitions	—	.50	.50	.25	.25	.50	—
Lectures	—	—	—	.50	.50	.50	.50
Minstrels	—	—	—	.50	.50	.50	.25
Pleasure gardens	.25	.50	—	—	—	—	—
Springs	—	1.00/day	1.00/day	1.50/day	1.50/day	1.50/day	2.00/day
Theater (box seat)	1.00	1.00	.75	.75	.75	.75	1.00
Theater (pit seat)	.50	.50	.50	.50	.50	.50	.75
Theater (gallery seat)	.25	.25	.25	.25	.25	.25	.50

Source: Advertisements in the *Baltimore American, Norfolk and Portsmouth Herald, Norfolk Virginian, Richmond Daily Compiler, Richmond Enquirer,* and *Richmond Whig.*

Resorts of Amusement and Status

nineteenth century. Box seats at the theater and visits to the springs were expensive throughout the century. The price of tickets for the circus and exhibitions varied, but they were always among the least expensive entertainments. The cost is more striking when ticket prices are compared with the cost of some common commodities or nineteenth-century wages. In 1850, for example, butter and coffee were approximately $0.10 per pound, while bacon was about $0.05 a pound in Baltimore. Stanley Lebergott indicates that the average daily wage of common laborers in Maryland and Virginia was $0.70 in 1850.[33] Thus, going to the springs was clearly not an option for laborers, and merely attending the circus or an exhibition meant spending an amount equivalent to five pounds of bacon or approximately one-third of a day's wages. That they continued to do so is itself testimony to the popularity of public amusements in the nineteenth century.

Although price differentials help explain why poorer citizens could not patronize some amusements, they do not explain why upper- and middle-class citizens stopped patronizing other amusements—amusements that gradually earned the reputation of being "lower class." In part, respectability was a key factor. From the beginning of the century some amusements were generally considered more proper than others. These amusements were usually educational and not detrimental to morals; museums and exhibitions are good examples. Church teachings were important in molding attitudes. Besides those amusements that had the church's seal of approval, there were also amusements that were respectable by the community's standards. In the early years of the century in Baltimore, Norfolk, and Richmond, conservative clergy did not, for example, approve of taverns, horse races, or the theater. Yet many people thought these activities respectable despite the clerical attitude.

For the upper class, however, respectability was always second to fashion. In the nineteenth-century South, that which was popular with the upper class was termed "fashionable." The word occurs frequently in newspapers, letters, and journals. Upper-class citizens, in fact, were often labeled "the fashionables." The editor of the *Baltimore American* was highly complimentary of the Baltimore Museum and the upper class when he noted in 1845 that the museum "still continues to be most liberally patronized by our fashionables" who composed "a refined audience."[34]

Upper-class Southerners often imitated the habits of aristocratic Europeans. This was known as "foreign fashion." In 1833 Christiana Lippincott of Baltimore wrote that she was tired of fancy balls because they were "too close an imitation of foreign fashion."[35] Masquerade balls were also European imports that appealed to many residents of Baltimore, Norfolk, and Richmond. Foreign visitors often commented on the irony of such emulation in a country that boasted about the absence of a hereditary upper class and the presence of political equality. Fashion, however, motivated much social activity.

Even as early as the 1820s, some amusements were more fashionable than others. The Baltimore Theatre and the Richmond Theatre, for example, always had community support and the support of the upper class. In contrast, although most people thought that the circus provided acceptable entertainment, going to the circus was never considered fashionable.[36] Minstrel shows briefly flirted with fashion but soon lost their appeal to the upper class. When the upper class withdrew support from a particular amusement, that amusement fell out of fashion. Likewise, when the upper class took up a new amusement, it soon became fashionable. Thus, for example, sporting clubs became fashionable after the middle of the century. When the upper class chose to attend particular theaters because of the type of shows that played there, these theaters were then considered the fashionable ones and upper-class citizens sought to be seen at them.

Fashion was capricious, but it was also often the consequence of many conscious choices. For various reasons at various times, upper-class citizens chose to withdraw their patronage, and thus their approval, from particular amusements. Sometimes, as in the case of visiting in taverns, the upper class's withdrawal was in response to bad associations—gambling and drunkenness—that the amusement had picked up. Similarly, the upper class's disengagement from public horse racing in the middle of the century was partly a response to loss of control over gambling and unruliness. While it could be argued that the negative associations had always been present in these amusements, what is important is the upper class's perception of them at a particular time and the reasons for this perception.

Those amusements that were valued primarily for their exclusiveness—social clubs, special social events, and summering at resorts—held out to patrons the possibility of ascribing to upper-class status merely by participation. In contrast to other amusements, the value of these amusements was not based on any positive cultural or educational contribution. Rather, these amusements were valued because they helped define the upper class. Because these amusements involved more expenditure of money or time than others, they distinguished the upper class in a period when that class felt its social position and control were being threatened by the upwardly mobile middle class.

There have been many attempts to explain how the consumptive aspect of leisure relates to social stratification. Sociologist Reuel Denney noted that in the nineteenth century, leisure demonstrated the division of labor. According to Denney, "the poorer man's leisure demonstrated his freedom from long hours of hard work; the rich man's leisure demonstrated the correctness of his consumption style."[37] Thorstein Veblen related the significance of leisure as a consumptive act to community size. He noted that when communities grew large, ostentatious display in leisure choices served to distinguish the upper class.[38]

In Baltimore, Norfolk, and Richmond upper-class citizens initially were distinguished from the general population by the amount of leisure time they had and how they spent it. As the century progressed, however, aspiring middle-class citizens—and even some of the self-improvement-oriented lower class—began to emulate the upper-class life-style. The upper class's response was to choose amusements that incorporated ostentatious displays of wealth. While conspicuous consumption of material goods expressed social standing, conspicuous consumption of amusement magnified social status, while separating the upper class from those below them. This, of course, reinforced social status by creating an exclusive social circle, making it easier for the elite to associate and marry with those of the same social rank at a time when urban growth made it more difficult to know everyone.

The leaders of the "fashionable crowd" were particularly interested in defining the proper upper-class life-style. John Neulinger and Miranda Breit have concluded that one of the primary functions of leisure in the twentieth century is that it offers "a basis for self-definition."[39] The evidence suggests that the use of leisure, particularly amusement choices, as a basis for self-definition was first adopted by a majority of the populations of Baltimore, Norfolk, and Richmond in the mid-nineteenth century. People went to amusements or joined clubs and associations with people who were like themselves. This self-definition, however, was not merely a matter of reinforcing personal values and priorities. Amusement choices also helped people define themselves in relation to their neighbors. Those who ascribed to a high social status through their amusement choices were often self-made or newly wealthy. Others were merely insecure and fearful that democracy was leading toward their loss of community control. In both instances amusement choices helped to secure positions in the upper class and cement social stratification.

By mid-century, amusements were divided along fairly strict class lines; social status, or desire for higher status, often played a major role in the determination of amusement choices. It should be noted, however, that the stratification of amusements mirrored the shifting relations between classes. The class system was dynamic, not static; thus, as class memberships shifted and notions of class changed, the stratification of amusements also shifted and changed. In fact, that mutability probably increased the significance of the role of amusement in expressing status.

Concurrent with the increase in stratification of amusements in these nineteenth-century cities was an increase in the receptivity and tolerance of amusements in general. In particular, hopes of securing status through amusement choices tended to mute most objections to the idea of amusement. Some amusements were still labeled "rough" or "lower-class." Amusements in general, however, no longer required educational or inspirational justification. Amusement itself was accepted as a given, and necessary, part of everyday life.

Conclusion

.. **I**n 1803 Eliza Morris, secretary of Baltimore's Impartial Humane Society, wrote a note of thanks to the Baltimore Theatre Corps. The Theatre corps had presented the society, an ecumenical organization of members from local Presbyterian, Catholic, Lutheran, Baptist, Swedenborgian New Church, and Dunkard congregations, a gift of $100, the proceeds of a benefit staged to raise money for the society's school. Speaking for the society, Morris implored the corps to "continue to play—until every destitute child of sorrow in the city, shall have ample means for food, clothing and education." A few days later, however, the society returned the gift, noting that the members appreciated the corps' intentions but were "truly sorry that the source of their humanity is founded on principles untenable and subversive of morality and virtue."[1] The society offered no explanation for its reversal.

During the nineteenth century, that sort of ambiguous stance toward amusements grew increasingly less common. Thus, by 1867 the editor of the *Norfolk Virginian* not only noted the changing attitudes toward amusement, he underscored the perception that a theater was an asset to a city: "A good theatre is a blessing to the trade of a city, and the fact should not be lost sight of by our citizens. There are indications that we are entering upon a new epoch,—we are beginning to conceive that mere toil, unrelieved by anything to gladden and adorn life, is not the only subject worthy the attention of an enlightened community."[2] The press's support of the theater was not new; what is significant about this statement is the recognition that attitudes had changed and that amusements were important to a city. The public was entering a new epoch in which it comprehended the value of amusements—not for refreshment but "to gladden and adorn life."

No doubt Eliza Morris would have found adornment an alien concept in this context, and it is likely that she never considered the relationship of the theater to her city's commercial development. That change came about gradually in the nineteenth century, although competition be-tween cities had existed since the eighteenth century. Baltimore, Nor-folk, and Richmond competed with each other, while Baltimore also competed with Philadelphia. Civic leaders were concerned with the image of their respective cities, hyping all signs of growth and develop-ment and emphasizing their competitors' weaknesses in order to attract business and trade. The weather and even the level of sickness in a particular area were judged to be indicators of how satisfactory the city would be as a commercial or manufacturing center. Thus, the yellow fever epidemic of 1855 proved to be a major setback for Norfolk not merely because of the deaths but because it hurt Norfolk's image at a time when it was competing fiercely with Baltimore and Richmond for business.[3] By the postwar period, city boosters had realized that the amusements in the city reflected its sophistication and could be used in promoting the city.

Baltimore had more working-class and immigrant organizations and clubs than Norfolk or Richmond, while Norfolk lagged behind in the number of available amusement options. Yet generally the responses to amusement in these three cities were similar. The evolution of amuse-ment in all three of them was continuous throughout the period 1800–1870; the Civil War did not alter the overall pattern. By the third quarter of the century, more people assumed that amusement and enter-tainment were synonymous—that amusements did not have to be edu-cational. Amusement itself was accepted as a part of everyday life. At the same time, there were more amusements, and there was more stratifica-tion of amusement participants. More people were using amusement choices as a means of expressing—and obtaining—social status. The distinction between high culture and popular culture grew clearer.

The underlying tensions had not disappeared; they had, however, been altered. Few people objected to pure entertainment or wanted amusements to be educational. Yet, there was still an undercurrent of belief that amusements had to be justified: they improved the city, made people happier and/or healthier, and were a good way to meet people in the increasingly impersonal urban areas. Ironically, people were in-creasingly less likely to meet all social classes and more likely to meet people like themselves in their amusements. The democratization of amusements of the early nineteenth century—however limited—had given way to a rhetoric of openness that reflected what would later be

Conclusion

called Social Darwinism. Amusements were open; but some were open only to those who could afford them, who could also meet membership qualifications, and who also knew the right people. The assumption was that everyone had an equal chance in life and those who did not make it merely had not tried hard enough.

Slavery, amusements, urban growth, and social stratification were intertwined in antebellum Baltimore, Norfolk, and Richmond. In addition to extolling local amusements, urban boosters encouraged the practice of hiring out slave laborers in factories as a means of achieving economic growth. As historians such as Ira Berlin and Richard Wade have noted, hiring out often accorded the leased slaves many freedoms their fellow bondsmen did not generally possess, including the freedom to participate in amusements.[4] Especially in Baltimore and Norfolk, where hiring out was fairly extensive, this practice fostered the development of grogshops and gambling parlors owned by free blacks and patronized by free blacks and slaves, as well as some lower-class whites. The altered status of these slaves led to more public regulation aimed at all slaves and free blacks. It reinforced the gentry's fear of losing control and appears to have been a factor in the stratification of amusements. The presence of slaves and free blacks in audiences contributed to the self-regulation of some public amusements such as theaters, exhibitions, gambling, and horse racing.

Upper-class citizens had a strong motivation for maintaining social stratification; they could achieve and even ascribe to status by virtue of their amusement choice. The new criteria for elite status included wealth, as well as ancestry. Thus, amusement choice was often used to declare wealth. This public declaration was also important for those in the upper-middle class who were aspiring to membership in "upper tendom" and often led to separate upper-class amusements that were distinguished by their lavish cost and exclusiveness. It also meant that the upper class gave a nod of approval to amusements in general, a factor that was of great importance in fostering the notion that amusements were necessary. When upper-class citizens neglected the community's traditional standards for fashion's sake, they had a wide following of imitators. Thus, they often changed attitudes toward particular amusements merely by their participation. In addition, both upper- and middle-class citizens put their mark of approval on amusements when they used them to help others—when, for example, they sponsored concerts to benefit the poor or excursions to take the poor for a day in the country. Although such efforts were neither so extensive or so well organized as those of the governing class of Victorian England, they did express the view that well-regulated amusements served an important function in society.[5]

While the wealthy continued to vie for social leadership, spokesmen within the growing middle class assumed cultural leadership. Some of this was overt—sermons or newspaper editorials, for example—but much was a matter of leadership by example. The middle class affixed its stamp of approval to the theater, exhibitions, museums, and lectures. The middle class's definition of gentility stressed temperance and industry, plus the wise use of leisure. By mid-century, some middle-class citizens were also indicating a concern that too much work, especially industrial labor, would be as harmful as idleness. Thus, in 1859 Baltimore's Mercantile Library Association sponsored a series of lectures that included discussion of the role of leisure in industrial society. The *Baltimore American* noted that one lecture, "The Social and Political Economy of Leisure," was a "plea for a well-employed leisure and a protest against that 'over-much work' which degrades the faculties and dulls the sensibilities."[6] Just as important for the long-run acceptance of the institution of amusement was the way that industrious workingmen combined amusement with instruction and benevolence in a variety of organizations. They used amusements to define proper behavior in much the same way that the upper class used amusements for social distinction. While the propriety of certain amusements that involved gambling or drinking was still questioned, amusement in general was established as an institution that was part of everyday life.

Locating the origins of popular amusements in the nineteenth century is not an easy task. It appears that much of what was popular with middle- and lower-class audiences was the result of the work of skillful promoters who were capable of gauging audience wants and then creating interest for their amusement offerings. Audience desires were the product of a number of factors. One thing that is clear is that an important consequence of the promotional work was extensive organization of popular public amusements—organization that paralleled the increasing organization of the workplace. Compared to his grandparents, the citizen of 1870 was more likely to pay for amusement that was packaged by someone who specialized in entertainment, and that

Conclusion

specialist probably resided in another city and provided similar entertainment to many localities.

By the mid-nineteenth century in Baltimore, Norfolk, and Richmond, the general agreement on the value of amusement coexisted with the division into separate amusement spheres. The distinction between high culture and popular culture grew sharper, and the division continued into the twentieth century and to the present. While fads or fashion may momentarily alter what happens to be popular with the general public, popular culture remains independent of high culture. Likewise, high culture continues to be strong and exclusive. One nineteenth-century development that is still important is the strong relationship between amusement cost and status. Many upper-class amusements still cost more than other amusements. Similarly, club membership and the access it affords also continue to be important; privilege breeds privilege, and sometimes money alone does not break down social barriers. Anyone with enough financial backing or credit may purchase a yacht, for example; but ownership does not automatically provide access to exclusive yacht clubs.

Another legacy of the nineteenth century is the awareness of the value of amusement in self-definition. Perhaps even more so than in the past, all sorts of people are cognizant that what they do, wear, eat, and drink for amusement says a lot about them—sometimes more than their work. Like their nineteenth-century ancestors, many Americans turn to amusements to express status, and some participate in particular amusements to achieve status. Taken to extremes, such self-consciousness may prove to be self-defeating, as the urge to impress others through amusement choices mitigates some of the value of amusement as a release from work. In fact, participating in the "right" amusement often becomes laborious as people "work" hard to have fun. As this study has shown, amusement choices may simultaneously serve a variety of purposes, some of which are far afield from amusement itself. A regrettable irony is that these purposes often take precedence over the pleasure that is essential for amusement.

Notes
·.·
Select Bibliography
·.·
Index
·.·

Abbreviations

BA	*Baltimore American and Commercial Daily Advertiser*
College of William and Mary	Earl Gregg Swem Library, College of William and Mary, Williamsburg, Va.
Duke Univ.	William R. Perkins Library, Duke University, Durham, N.C.
Md. Hist. Soc.	Maryland Historical Society, Baltimore
NPH	*Norfolk and Portsmouth Herald*
NV	*Norfolk Virginian*
RDC	*Daily Compiler and Richmond Commercial Register*
RE	*Richmond Enquirer*
RW	*Richmond Whig*
UNC Lib.	University of North Carolina Library, Chapel Hill
UVA Library	University of Virginia Library, Charlottesville
Va. Hist. Soc.	Virginia Historical Society, Richmond
Va. State Lib.	Virginia State Library, Richmond

Notes

••• Introduction •••

1. Michel Chevalier, *Society, Manners, and Politics in the United States: Letters on North America,* ed. John William Ward (Ithaca, N.Y., 1969), p. 305. In *Sportsmen and Gamesmen* (Boston, 1981), pp. 1–21, John Dizikes describes the transformation of the inherited aristocratic sporting tradition into a popular form in the United States, noting how democracy molded popular amusements. I put more emphasis on the longing for hierarchy that existed alongside the democratic urges; generally, I locate the desire for hierarchy in the upper class, who most benefited from the maintenance of such order in the Upper South.

2. Dale A. Somers, *The Rise of Sports in New Orleans, 1850–1900* (Baton Rouge, La., 1972), p. 73.

3. For discussions of leisure, see Josef Pieper, *Leisure, the Basis of Culture* (New York, 1952); Joffre Dumazedier, *Toward a Society of Leisure,* trans. Stewart E. McClure (New York, 1967); Richard Kraus, *Recreation and Leisure in Modern Society* (New York, 1972); Max Kaplan, *Leisure in America: A Social Inquiry* (New York, 1960).

4. Thomas Charlton Henry, *An Inquiry into the Consistency of Popular Amusements with a Profession of Christianity* (Charleston, S.C., 1825), p. 104.

5. Rev. J. T. Crane, *Popular Amusements* (Cincinnati, 1869), p. 32.

6. *BA,* 1 Jan. 1831, 15 Mar. 1813. The *RE,* for example, began regularly using *"Amusements"* as a column heading in 1858; *"Summer Retreats"* was also given a heading in June 1858.

7. Frederic W. Sawyer, *A Plea for Amusements* (New York, 1847), p. 16.

8. James Leonard Corning, *The Christian Law of Amusement* (Buffalo, 1859), pp. 9–10.

9. Hess to Mrs. Swift Miller, 18 Feb. 1849, Wooster Papers, Southern Historical Collection, UNC Lib. See also Harriet Augusta Caskie Scott to Fannie Johnson, 14 Feb. 1848, Frances Jean Johnson Caskie Papers, Va. Hist. Soc.

10. Lucretia VanBibber to Anne C. Coleman, 8 Nov. 1834, Anne Caroline Coleman Papers, Md. Hist. Soc.

11. Jacob Frey, *Reminiscences of Baltimore* (Baltimore, 1893), p. 57.

12. Alonzo May, "Dramatic Encyclopedia" (1906), Alonzo May Papers, microfilm (8 reels), Md. Hist. Soc., reel 1, B13-1810.

13. *RE,* 17 Sept. 1819. See also *RE,* 7 Dec. 1819, 28 Nov. 1829; May, "Dramatic Encyclopedia," reel 2, B14-1830.

14. *BA,* 1 Jan. 1831.

15. George W. Munford to Dr. Robert Munford, 26 Dec. 1842, Munford-Ellis Papers, Duke Univ.

16. William B. Wood, *Personal Recollections of the Stage, Embracing Notices of Actors, Authors, and Auditors* (Philadelphia, 1855), p. 457.

17. *RE,* 2 June 1863.

18. *NV,* 1 Apr. 1867.

19. Sawyer, *A Plea for Amusements,* pp. 159, 242.

20. See Daniel R. Hundley, *Social Relations in Our Southern States,* ed. William J. Cooper, Jr. (1860; rept., Baton Rouge, La., 1979).

21. See Daniel T. Rodgers, *The Work Ethic in Industrial America, 1850–1920* (Chicago, 1978); Donald J. Mrozek, *Sport and American Mentality, 1880–1910* (Knoxville, Tenn., 1983); Stephen Hardy, *How Boston Played: Sport, Recreation, and Community, 1865–1915* (Boston, 1982); Roy Rosenzweig, *Eight Hours for What We Will: Workers and Leisure in an Industrial City, 1870–1920* (Cambridge, Eng., 1983); Francis G. Couvares, *The Remaking of Pittsburgh: Class and Culture in an Industrializing City, 1877–1919* (Albany, 1984); Steven J. Ross, *Workers on the Edge: Work, Leisure, and Politics in Industrializing Cincinnati, 1788–1890* (New York, 1985); Stephen Hardy and Alan G. Ingham, "Games, Structures, and Agency: Historians on the American Play Movement," *Journal of Social History* 17 (Fall 1983): 285–301.

22. In fact, I tend to agree with Gareth Stedman Jones's belief that leisure can be overpoliticized "as an arena of struggle" ("Class Expression versus Social Control? A Critique of Recent Trends in the Social History of 'Leisure,' " *History Workshop* 4 [Autumn 1977]: 162–70).

••• Chapter One •••

1. Quoted in Jesse Lyman Hurlbut, *The Story of Chautauqua* (New York, 1921), p. 184.

2. See *BA,* 16 Jan. 1849, 1 June 1865.

3. Richard M. Bernard, "A Portrait of Baltimore in 1800: Economic and Occupational Patterns in an Early American City," *Maryland Historical Magazine* 69 (1974): 345; Sherry H. Olson, *Baltimore: The Building of an American City* (Baltimore, 1980), p. 83.

4. Clayton Colman Hall, *Baltimore: Its History and Its People* (New York, 1912), p. 63; George H. Elmer, "Reminiscences of Federal Hill in 1886," *Baltimore Magazine* (May 1952), quoted in Norman G. Rukert, *Federal Hill: A Baltimore National Historic District* (Baltimore, 1980), p. 83; Olson, *Baltimore,* p. 85; Hugh Murray, *Historical Account of Discoveries and Travels in North America,* 2 vols. (London, 1829), 2:415; Henry M. Brackenridge, *Recollections of Persons and Places in the West* (Philadelphia, 1834), p. 157; Sir Charles Augustus Murray, *Travels in North America during the Years 1834, 1835, and 1836,* 2 vols. (London, 1839), 2:290; Francis F. Beirne, *The Amiable Baltimoreans* (New York, 1951), p. 286.

5. Quoted in Olson, *Baltimore,* p. 115. See also Hamilton Owens, *Baltimore on the Chesapeake* (Garden City, N.Y., 1941), p. 328; F. Barham Zincke, *Last Winter in the United States* (London, 1868), pp. 32–33; Francis Hall, *Travels in Canada, and*

Notes

the *United States, in 1816 and 1817* (Boston, 1818), p. 194; Henry B. Fearon, *Sketches of America* (London, 1818), p. 343; Thomas Hamilton, *Men and Manners in America*, 2 vols. (Edinburgh, 1833), 2:14; Bernard, "A Portrait of Baltimore in 1800," p. 360.

6. Mrs. Matilda C. Houstoun, *Hesperos; or, Travels in the West*, 2 vols. (London, 1850), 1:227; Gabriel Paul Othein de Cleron, comte d'Haussonville, *A travers les Etats-Unis, notes et impressions* (Paris, 1883), pp. 89–90; George W. Howard, *The Monumental City, Its Past History and Present Resources* (Baltimore, 1873), p. 35; J. S. Buckingham, Esq., *America, Historical, Statistic, and Descriptive*, 2 vols. (New York, 1841), 1:266; John H. B. Latrobe, "Reminiscences of Baltimore in 1824," *Maryland Historical Magazine* 1 (June 1906): 116; Ira Berlin, *Slaves without Masters: The Free Negro in the Antebellum South* (New York, 1974), p. 258.

7. Bernard, "A Portrait of Baltimore in 1800," p. 351.

8. Beirne, *The Amiable Baltimoreans*, p. 142; Owens, *Baltimore on the Chesapeake*, pp. 245–49; John H. Hewitt, *Shadows on the Wall; or, Glimpses of the Past* (Baltimore, 1877), p. 54; Hall, *Baltimore*, p. 158; H. E. Shepherd, ed., *History of Baltimore, Maryland, from Its Founding as a Town to the Current Year, 1729–1898* (Uniontown, Pa., 1898), p. 107; Chevalier, *Society, Manners, and Politics*, p. 390; *BA*, 16 Feb. 1857.

9. William S. Forrest, *Historical and Descriptive Sketches of Norfolk and Vicinity* (Philadelphia, 1853), pp. 340–41; Lelia Skipwith Carter Tucker to Mrs. Cornelia L. Littlefield, 11 May 1825, Tucker-Coleman Collection, College of William and Mary; Francis Baily, *Journal of a Tour in Unsettled Parts of North America, in 1796 and 1797* (London, 1856), pp. 104–5; R. Owen to Dr. John Owen, 29 July 1813, Campbell Family Papers, Duke Univ.

10. Anne Royall, *The Black Book; or, a Continuation of Travels in the United States*, 3 vols. (Washington, D.C., 1828–29), 1:254.

11. Thomas J. Wertenbaker, *Norfolk: Historic Southern Port* (Durham, N.C., 1931), pp. 143–46.

12. Margaret Hunter Hall, *The Aristocratic Journey: Being the Outspoken Letters of Mrs. Basil Hall Written during a Fourteen Months' Sojourn in America, 1827–1828* (New York and London, 1931), p. 198; Chevalier, *Society, Manners, and Politics*, pp. 314–15; John James Audubon, *Letters of John James Audubon*, 2 vols. (Boston, 1930), 1:139, 2:254.

13. George William Featherstonhaugh, *Excursion through the Slave States* (New York, 1844), p. 162.

14. Lewis Mattison, "Life of the Town," in *Richmond, Capital of Virginia* (Richmond, 1938), pp. 29–58; Marie Tyler-McGraw and Gregg D. Kimball, *In Bondage and Freedom: Antebellum Black Life in Richmond, Virginia* (Richmond, 1988), p. 12; Virginius Dabney, *Richmond: The Story of a City* (Garden City, N.Y., 1976), p. 113.

15. Chevalier, *Society, Manners, and Politics*, p. 316; Michael B. Chesson, *Richmond after the War, 1865–1890* (Richmond, 1981), pp. 4, 9.

16. Chesson, *Richmond after the War*, pp. 9, 15.

17. John W. M. Williams, Diary, 28 Aug. 1855, John W. M. Williams Papers,

Notes

Southern Historical Collection, UNC Lib.; William H. Nash to G. W. Johnson, 3 Nov. 1855, George Wesley Johnson Papers, Duke Univ.; Charles Shield to Charles W. Dabney, 17 Nov. 1855, Charles W. Dabney Papers, Southern Historical Collection, UNC Lib.; Wertenbaker, *Norfolk,* pp. 208–16; and H. W. Burton, *The History of Norfolk, Virginia: A Review of Important Events and Incidents Which Occurred from 1763 to 1877* (Norfolk, 1877), pp. 23–24.

18. J. F. McMullen to Mr. Clark, 6 Sept. 1855, McMullen Family Papers, Duke Univ.

19. May, "Dramatic Encyclopedia," reel 1, 1797-B2, reel 2, B6-1816.

20. Latrobe, "Reminiscences of Baltimore," p. 123.

21. Mary Boykin Chesnut, *A Diary from Dixie,* ed. Isabella D. Martin and Myrta Lockett Avary (Gloucester, Mass., 1961), p. 299. See also Sallie Ann Brock Putnam, *Richmond during the War: Four Years of Personal Observation, by a Richmond Lady* (New York, 1867), p. 81.

22. John P. Little, *Richmond, the Capital of Virginia: Its History* (Richmond, 1851), pp. 106–7.

23. David R. Goldfield, *Urban Growth in the Age of Sectionalism: Virginia, 1847–1861* (Baton Rouge, La., 1977), pp. 34, 50.

24. Miss Mendell, *Notes of Travel and Life* (New York, 1854), p. 161.

25. Quoted in Arthur Charles Cole, *The Irrepressible Conflict, 1850–1865* (New York, 1934), p. 399.

26. John Langbourne Williams to Maria Ward Williams, 8 Apr. 1867, Williams Family Papers, Va. Hist. Soc.

27. David Campbell to Claiborne W. Gooch, 16 July 1818, Gooch Family Papers, Va. Hist. Soc. Robert P. Sutton describes this anxiety and gives numerous examples in "Nostalgia, Pessimism, and Malaise: The Doomed Aristocrat in Late-Jeffersonian Virginia," *Virginia Magazine of History and Biography* 76 (Jan. 1968): 41–55.

28. See Hardy, *How Boston Played*; Rosenzweig, *Eight Hours for What We Will*; Couvares, *The Remaking of Pittsburgh*; Ross, *Workers on the Edge*; Olson, *Baltimore,* pp. 118–20; Berlin, *Slaves without Masters,* pp. 54–55, 231, 237.

29. Samuel Mordecai, *Virginia, Especially Richmond, in By-Gone Days* (Richmond, 1860), pp. 359–60; John T. O'Brien, "Factory, Church, and Community: Blacks in Antebellum Richmond," *Journal of Southern History* 44 (Nov. 1978): 510–14; Berlin, *Slaves without Masters,* p. 318.

30. Stephen Davis, *Notes of a Tour in America, in 1832 and 1833* (Edinburgh, 1833), p. 106.

31. Andrew Reed, *A Narrative of the Visit to the American Churches,* 2 vols. (London, 1835), 1:260.

32. Mendell, *Notes,* p. 170.

33. *The North American Tourist* (New York, 1839), p. 405; Buckingham, *America,* 1:183; Chesson, *Richmond after the War,* p. 18.

34. See Max Kaplan, *Leisure: Theory and Policy* (New York, 1975), pp. 89, 235.

35. Linnaeus to Mrs. Francis Y. Custis, 9 June 1830, John Beauchamp Jones Papers, Southern Historical Collection, UNC Lib.

Notes

36. Lucretia VanBibber to Anne C. Coleman, 8 July 1833, Anne Caroline Coleman Papers, Md. Hist. Soc.

37. Mrozek, *Sport and American Mentality,* p. 231.

·· **Chapter Two** ··

1. John M. Duncan, *Travels through Part of the United States and Canada in 1818 and 1819* (New York, 1823), pp. 232–33. See also Frey, *Reminiscences,* p. 49; Forrest, *Historical and Descriptive Sketches,* p. 158; Wertenbaker, *Norfolk,* p. 139; W. H. T. Squires, *Historical Norfolk, 1636–1936,* Book 1 of *Through the Years in Norfolk* (Portsmouth, Va., 1937), p. 52; W. Asbury Christian, *Richmond, Her Past and Present* (Richmond, 1912), pp. 109, 211; Harry M. Ward, *Richmond: An Illustrated History* (Northridge, Calif., 1985), pp. 88–89.

2. Ward, *Richmond,* p. 88; Frey, *Reminiscences,* p. 49; Squires, *Historical Norfolk,* p. 52.

3. Ward, *Richmond,* pp. 88–89.

4. *BA,* 2 June 1817. See also Richard D. Altick, *The Shows of London* (Cambridge, Mass., 1978).

5. For advertisements, see *BA,* 1 July 1815, 1 Apr. 1819, 1 Oct. 1827, 2 Sept. 1833, 1 Mar. 1851, 15 Nov. 1861.

6. *BA,* 15 Apr. 1829. See also *BA,* 1 Feb. 1811; *NPH,* 1 Jan. 1821.

7. *BA,* 2 Oct. 1815. See also *BA,* 15 Feb. 1813; *NPH,* 2 July 1819; *RE,* 15 Dec. 1804, 3 Feb. 1810, 19 Jan. 1811.

8. *BA,* 1 Sept. 1825, 1 Aug. 1813.

9. Owens, *Baltimore on the Chesapeake,* p. 216; Thomas Waters Griffith, *Annals of Baltimore* (Baltimore, 1824), p. 208.

10. *BA,* 1 Jan. 1827. See also *Norfolk Gazette and Public Ledger,* quoted in Wertenbaker, *Norfolk,* p. 129; *RE,* 1 Nov. 1811, 3 Jan. 1828; *BA,* 15 Feb. 1811, 1 Mar. 1819, 1 Mar., 2 July, 15 Dec. 1821, 1 July 1823, 15 July 1831; May, "Dramatic Encyclopedia," reel 6, P21-1841.

11. *NPH,* 23 Jan., 2 Feb. 1802. See also *RE,* 3 Jan. 1824; Lucretia to Anne C. Coleman, 9 Dec. 1831, Anne Caroline Coleman Papers, Md. Hist. Soc.

12. Fearon, *Sketches of America,* p. 295.

13. J. J. Moorman to Mrs. Moorman, 11 Oct. 1829, in John J. Moorman, "My Mother. A Memento of the Life, and Character, of Mrs. Martha Jane Moorman: Together with a part of her Correspondence. Compiled for the use of her Children" (Harrisonburg, 20 May 1835), in the collection of Jerry Showalter, Ivy, Va.

14. *RE,* 19 Jan. 1811.

15. *NPH,* 3 Dec. 1827.

16. *BA,* 1 Oct. 1829.

17. Mordecai, *Virginia, Especially Richmond, in By-Gone Days,* p. 344.

18. *BA,* 15 Feb. 1817, 1 Apr. 1823, 1 May 1835.

19. Reed, *Narrative,* 1:302.

20. "Mrs. Flora Byrne's Reminiscence of 1830," quoted in May, "Dramatic Encyclopedia," reel 2, B39-1830.

21. *BA*, 16 Mar. 1835.

22. *RW*, 1 May 1835.

23. Margarette to Mr. William M. Gibson, 26 Mar. 1835, John Gibson Letters, Grundy-Gibson Papers, Md. Hist. Soc.

24. *BA*, 4 Nov. 1831. See also *BA*, 1 July 1833; *RE*, 15 Nov. 1855.

25. *BA*, 15 Feb. 1841.

26. *BA*, 15 Sept. 1863, 1 Nov. 1867; *RE*, 16 Apr. 1867, 15 Nov. 1855. See also Neil Harris, *Humbug: The Art of P. T. Barnum* (Boston, 1973), p. 49; Leslie Fiedler, *Freaks: Myths and Images of the Secret Self* (New York, 1978).

27. *BA*, 1 July 1851.

28. *BA*, 15 Apr. 1869.

29. *BA*, 1 Nov. 1869.

30. *RE*, 17 Jan. 1851. For the stir created by a clairvoyant little girl in Richmond in 1845, see Elizabeth Selden Maclurg Wickham to Littleton Waller Tazewell Wickham, Nov. 1845, Wickham Letters, Valentine Museum, Richmond.

31. May, "Dramatic Encyclopedia," reel 6, P1-1830.

32. *BA*, 1 Jan. 1845; Joseph Pickering, *Inquiries of an Emigrant: Being the Narrative of an English Farmer from the Years 1824 to 1830* (London, 1832), p. 44.

33. May, "Dramatic Encyclopedia," reel 6, P1-1830; *RE*, 2 Mar. 1847.

34. Anne R. Sherrard to Col. George W. Munford, 13 Sept. 1842, Munford-Ellis Papers, Duke Univ.

35. Forrest, *Historical and Descriptive Sketches*, p. 225.

36. *Richmond Examiner*, 21 Aug. 1849, quoted in Watkins Norvell, *Richmond, Virginia: Colonial, Revolutionary, and Confederate, and the Present, 1896* (Richmond, 1896), n.p.; *Norfolk Argus*, 17 Sept. 1849, quoted in Wertenbaker, *Norfolk*, p. 129. See also Alexander Wilbourne Weddell, *Richmond, Virginia, in Old Prints, 1737–1887* (Richmond, 1932), p. 228; Christian, *Richmond*, p. 165.

37. Elizabeth Seldon Maclurg Wickham to Littleton Waller Tazewell Wickham, 3 Mar. 1853, Wickham Letters, Valentine Museum.

38. Agnes Bondurant, *Poe's Richmond* (Richmond, 1942), p. 15.

39. Quoted in Carl Bode, *The American Lyceum: Town Meeting of the Mind* (New York, 1956), p. 251.

40. *NPH*, 4 May 1835.

41. Bode, *The American Lyceum*, p. 149; John P. Kennedy, *Address Delivered before the Maryland Institute for the Promotion of the Mechanic Arts* (Baltimore, 1851), p. 28; Howard, *The Monumental City*, pp. 41–42.

42. Bode, *The American Lyceum*, p. 149; *BA*, 1 May 1857.

43. *RE*, 18 Jan., 15 Apr. 1859.

44. *BA*, 1 Apr. 1865.

45. Harris, *Humbug*, p. 291, discusses the differences between the museum and the circus in terms of instruction versus entertainment.

46. *RE*, 4 Nov. 1823, 3 Nov. 1843, 18 Sept. 1849, 18 Feb. 1851; Robert I. Vexler, comp. and ed., *Baltimore: A Chronological and Documentary History* (Dobbs Ferry, N.Y., 1975), p. 34.

47. Christian, *Richmond*, p. 190; *RE*, 1 Nov. 1853, 18 Sept. 1857; Burton, *History*

Notes

of Norfolk, pp. 16, 26, 35; Norvell Winsboro Wilson Diary, 29 May 1871, 2 Nov. 1871, Norvell Winsboro Wilson Papers, Southern Historical Collection, UNC Lib.

48. Harris, *Humbug,* p. 108; *RE,* 16 Nov. 1849; Carl Bode, *The Anatomy of American Popular Culture, 1840–1861* (Berkeley, Calif., 1959), pp. 35–36.

49. Frey, *Reminiscences,* pp. 81–82.

50. Austin Dall to Mary Brand, 25 Feb. 1851, Mary Brand Dall Correspondence, Duke Univ.

51. Harris, *Humbug,* pp. 137–38.

52. Phineas Taylor Barnum, *Struggles and Triumphs: or, Forty Years' Recollections of P. T. Barnum* (rept., New York, 1930), pp. 193–94.

53. Fritz Redlich, "Leisure-Time Activities: A Historical, Sociological, and Economic Analysis," *Explorations in Entrepreneurial History,* 2d ser., 3 (Fall 1965): 3–24.

54. Barnum, *Struggles and Triumphs,* pp. 84, 473; M. R. Werner, *Barnum* (New York, 1923), p. 319.

••• **Chapter Three** •••

1. Martha Clark, *Victims of Amusements* (Philadelphia, 1849), p. 40; Bryan Akers, ed., *Graphic Description of the Burning of the Richmond Theatre, December 26, 1811* (Lynchburg, Va., 1879), pp. 3, 7. See also *Full Account of the Richmond Theatre Fire* (Richmond, 1858), p. 30; Christian, *Richmond,* pp. 78–79; Martin Staples Shockley, *The Richmond Stage, 1784–1812* (Charlottesville, Va., 1977), pp. 360–82.

2. In addition to Shockley, see Dabney, *Richmond,* p. 91; *American Standard,* 1 Jan. 1812, quoted in *Full Account of the Burning of the Richmond Theatre,* p. 23.

3. *Calamity at Richmond* (Philadelphia, 1812), xi; Little, *Richmond,* p. 124; *Full Account of the Richmond Theatre Fire,* p. 14; Archibald Alexander, *A Discourse Occasioned by the Burning of the Theatre in the City of Richmond, Va., on the Twenty-sixth of December, 1811* (Philadelphia, 1812), p. 15.

4. James Dormon notes that all available sources suggest that theater audiences of the Old South did not differ from their Northern counterparts (*Theater in the Antebellum South, 1815–1861* [Chapel Hill, N.C., 1967], p. 251). See also Harris, *Humbug,* p. 36.

5. May, "Dramatic Encyclopedia," reel 1, B6-1816.

6. Joanne L. Gatewood, ed., "Richmond during the Virginia Constitutional Convention of 1829–1830: An Extract from the Diary of Thomas Green, October 1, 1829, to January 31, 1830," *Virginia Magazine of History and Biography* 84 (July 1976): 304; *RDC,* 2 Nov. 1829.

7. Fanny Booth to Hester E. VanBibber, 28 Aug. 1820, Frances Amanda Booth Taliaferro Letters, Va. Hist. Soc.

8. Hall, *The Aristocratic Journey,* p. 163.

9. *Mercantile Advertiser,* 13 July 1821; May, "Dramatic Encyclopedia," reel 2, B44-1811.

10. May, "Dramatic Encyclopedia," reel 1, B3-1811.

11. Hewitt, *Shadows on the Wall,* pp. 113–14.

12. May, "Dramatic Encyclopedia," reel 11, no. 6, p. 14; Martin Staples Shockley, "A History of the Theatre in Richmond, Virginia, 1819–1838" (Ph.D. diss., University of North Carolina, 1938), p. 65.

13. *RDC,* 10 Nov. 1819, quoted in Shockley, "A History of the Theatre," p. 65. For an advertisement specifically mentioning mulattoes, see *RE,* 14 Nov. 1838.

14. Advertisements in the *BA, NV,* and *RE* from 1800 to 1870; Stanley Lebergott, *The Americans: An Economic Record* (New York, 1984), esp. pp. 129, 131–32, 154, 222.

15. See Dizikes, *Sportsmen and Gamesmen,* esp. pp. 1–21.

16. *Virginia Patriot, and Richmond Daily Mercantile Advertiser,* 3 Mar. 1818, in Edwin V. Valentine Notes, Valentine Museum; *RE,* 17 Jan. 1851. See also John Thomas Scharf, *History of Baltimore City and County,* rev. ed., 2 vols. (Philadelphia, 1971), 2:695.

17. See *BA,* 15 Dec. 1817, 1 Dec. 1831, 15 Mar. 1841, 1 Mar. 1844, 1 Jan. 1855; May, "Dramatic Encyclopedia," reel 2, B33-1829, reel 3, 1853-5.

18. Fearon, *Sketches of America,* p. 86. See also David Grimsted, *Melodrama Unveiled: American Theater and Culture, 1800–1850* (Chicago, 1968), p. 52; Latrobe, "Reminiscences of Baltimore," p. 121.

19. C. B. Parsons, *The Pulpit and the Stage; or, The Two Itinerancies. An Historic, Biographic, Philosophic Miscellany* (Nashville, 1860), p. 59.

20. Wood, *Personal Recollections,* p. 341.

21. May, "Dramatic Encyclopedia," reel 1, B4-1805, B5-1805.

22. Ibid., reel 1, no. 7, pp. 95–96, 115, B2-1804, B3-1804. See also *BA,* 1 May 1811.

23. See Dormon, *Theater in the Ante Bellum South,* pp. 231–51. Patriotic plays and songs also provoked wild cheering.

24. *NPH,* 15 Apr. 1803.

25. May, "Dramatic Encyclopedia," reel 1, B21-1813, reel 2, B3-1826; Edward T. Coke, *A Subaltern's Furlough: Descriptive of Scenes in Various Parts of the United States, Upper and Lower Canada* (London, 1833), p. 74; Charles Richard Weld, *A Vacation Tour in the United States and Canada* (London, 1855), p. 624. See also *RE,* 3 Jan. 1851.

26. Charles William Janson, *The Stranger in America: Containing Observations Made during a Long Residence in That Country* (London, 1807), pp. 256–57.

27. Count Francesco Arese, *A Trip to the Prairies and in the Interior of North America, 1837–1838,* trans. Andrew Evans (New York, 1934), pp. 12–13.

28. *RE,* 18 May 1847.

29. May, "Dramatic Encyclopedia," reel 1, B4-1815.

30. Ibid., reel 2, B5-1826, B6-1826, B7-1826.

31. Hewitt, *Shadows on the Wall,* p. 107; Scharf, *History of Baltimore City and County,* 2:694.

32. Meade Minnigerode, *The Fabulous Forties, 1840–1850* (New York, 1924), p. 206; Arthur Hornblow, *A History of the Theatre in America,* 2 vols. (Phila-

Notes

delphia, 1919), 2:38–42; Robert Toll, *Blacking Up: The Minstrel Show in Nineteenth-Century America* (New York, 1974), pp. 16–17.

33. May, "Dramatic Encyclopedia," reel 2, B5-1826.

34. Parsons, *The Pulpit and the Stage*, p. 61; Crane, *Popular Amusements*, p. 49.

35. May, "Dramatic Encyclopedia," reel 2, B3-1826.

36. Ibid., reel 2, P2-1830.

37. Quoted in Shockley, "A History of the Theatre," p. 66n. See also May, "Dramatic Encyclopedia," reel 2, B12-1825.

38. May, "Dramatic Encyclopedia," reel 2, B4-1828, B5-1828.

39. Wood, *Personal Recollections*, p. 323.

40. Parsons, *The Pulpit and the Stage*, p. 74; May, "Dramatic Encyclopedia," reel 1, B4-1805, B5-1805.

41. *NPH*, 24 Mar. 1803.

42. William Dunlap, *A History of the American Theatre* (New York, 1832), p. 211.

43. *BA*, 2 July 1827, 2 Feb. 1857; *RE*, 15 June 1847; May, "Dramatic Encyclopedia," reel 7, RA5-1846. See also Scharf, *History of Baltimore City and County*, 2:695.

44. Parsons, *The Pulpit and the Stage*, p. 60.

45. Claudia D. Johnson, "That Guilty Third Tier: Prostitution in Nineteenth-Century American Theaters," in *Victorian America*, ed. Daniel Walker Howe (Philadelphia, 1976), p. 120.

46. May, "Dramatic Encyclopedia," reel 2, B6-1821, reel 5, F10-1829. Examples of advertisements may be found in *BA*, 1 June 1827, 15 May 1833, 2 Feb., 15 Oct. 1835, 1 Apr., 15 June 1839, 2 Oct. 1843; *NPH*, 4 Mar. 1833; *RE*, 2 Apr. 1847.

47. "Rules and Regulations of the Richmond Theatre," Broadside, Vertical Files, Valentine Museum.

48. Hornblow, *A History of the Theatre in America*, 1:251.

49. Ibid., 1:257.

50. Shockley, "A History of the Theatre," p. 136.

51. *RE*, 6 Jan. 1810.

52. May, "Dramatic Encyclopedia," reel 1, B1-1812; Hornblow, *A History of the Theatre in America*, 2:60–61; Minnigerode, *The Fabulous Forties*, p. 145.

53. Mary Caroline Crawford, *The Romance of the American Theatre* (New York, 1940), p. 395; Henry Anthony Murray, *Lands of the Slave and the Free; or, Cuba, the United States, and Canada*, 2d ed. (London, 1857), p. 199.

54. Terry Theodore, "The Confederate Theatre: The Confederate Drama," *Lincoln Herald* 77 (Spring 1975), p. 33; Shockley, "A History of the Theatre," pp. 167, 181. An announcement in the *RE* for 2 Feb. 1847 indicated that the Richmond Theatre would soon reopen under the management of E. A. Marshall, formerly of Walnut Street Theatre, Philadelphia, and Holliday Street Theatre, Baltimore.

55. May, "Dramatic Encyclopedia," reel 2, B8-1823.

56. *BA*, 15 May 1865; *NV*, 1 Dec. 1875; *RE*, 2 Apr. 1841, 1 Mar., 1 Apr. 1853, 3 Dec. 1861. See also Hall, *Baltimore*, p. 152; May, "Dramatic Encyclopedia," reel

7, HA32-1854; Burton, *History of Norfolk,* pp. 31, 183; "Music and the Theatre" (1937), TS, Va. Hist. Soc.

57. Minnigerode, *The Fabulous Forties,* p. 30; Hornblow, *A History of the Theatre in America,* 2:143.

58. Shockley, "A History of the Theatre," p. 238; John Pendleton Kennedy, *At Home and Abroad* (New York, 1872), p. 175.

59. May, "Dramatic Encyclopedia," reel 2, B3-1840, B4-1840; *RE,* 16 Jan. 1810; Wood, *Personal Recollections,* pp. 304, 353; Frances Trollope, *Domestic Manners of the Americans,* 2 vols. (London, 1832), 1:297; Buckingham, *America,* 1:281.

60. Shockley, "A History of the Theatre," p. 194.

61. Tyrone Power, *Impressions of America during the Years 1833, 1834, and 1835,* 2 vols. (London, 1836), 1:141.

62. May, "Dramatic Encyclopedia," reel 5, FT12-1830.

63. *BA,* 1 June 1839.

64. *BA,* 1 Mar. 1855; James H. Dormon, "Thespis in Dixie: Professional Theater in Confederate Richmond," *Virginia Cavalcade* 28 (Summer 1978): 6; Terry Theodore, "The Confederate Theatre: Richmond: Theatre Capital of the Confederacy," *Lincoln Herald* 77 (Fall 1975): 162; John Ross Dix, *Transatlantic Tracings; or, Sketches of Persons and Scenes in America* (London, 1853), p. 229.

65. *BA,* 1 Apr. 1861.

66. *BA,* 15 Feb. 1853.

67. Scharf, *History of Baltimore City and County,* 2:693; Hall, *Baltimore,* p. 228.

68. May, "Dramatic Encyclopedia," reel 7, R17-1862; Scharf, *History of Baltimore City and County,* 2:693; Meredith Janvier, *Baltimore in the 80's and 90's* (Baltimore, 1933), p. 51.

69. *BA,* 16 Oct. 1843. See also *BA,* 15 Nov. 1845, for references to attendance "by the beauty and fashion of the city." *BA,* 13 Dec. 1843, lists admission prices as box, $0.50; pit, $0.25; upper boxes and "colored gallery," $0.25. These prices were typical.

70. Toll, *Blacking Up,* pp. 18, 57; *BA,* 1 Jan., 15 Jan., 15 Mar. 1853; *RE,* 16 Sept. 1853, 1 Feb. 1859. For advertisements of the newly opened Kunkle's Ethiopian Opera House, see *BA,* 2 Sept., 15 Oct. 1861.

71. "In Torn Tights," n.p., n.d., clipping, Harvard Theatre Collection, quoted in Toll, *Blacking Up,* p. 138.

72. *NV,* 2 Oct. 1877.

73. Terry Theordore, "The Confederate Theatre: Theatre Personalities and Practices during the Confederacy," *Lincoln Herald* 76 (Winter 1974): 187.

74. Quoted, ibid. See also Theodore, "The Confederate Theatre: Richmond," p. 163; Dormon, "Thespis in Dixie," pp. 10, 12.

75. Terry Theodore, "The Confederate Theatre in the Deep South," *Lincoln Herald* 77 (Summer 1975): 102; Theodore, "The Confederate Theatre: The Confederate Drama," p. 33.

76. Theodore, "The Confederate Theatre: Richmond," p. 162. The Richmond Theatre burned on January 1, 1862, and the company moved to Franklin Hall,

Notes

where it was renamed Richmond Varieties. A new Richmond Theatre was built and opened in February 1863.

77. Ibid., pp. 162–63; Dormon, "Thespis in Dixie," p. 7. See also Theodore, "The Confederate Theatre: Theatre Personalities and Practices," pp. 189, 192.

78. Alexander Wilbourne Weddell, *Richmond, Virginia, in Old Prints,* p. 231. For a similar description, see Chesnut, *A Diary from Dixie,* p. 286.

79. Hess to Mrs. Swift Miller, 18 Feb. 1849, Wooster Papers, Southern Historical Collection, UNC Lib.; Mrs. Christian to Richard Christian, 29 Mar. 1866, Christian Family Papers, College of William and Mary, quoted in Chesson, *Richmond after the War,* p. 82.

80. *BA,* 15 Apr. 1869. See also *BA,* 15 Mar. 1865; *NV,* 1 Mar. 1867; *RW,* 16 Mar. 1869, 5 Dec. 1871.

81. *NV,* 15 Apr. 1869. For a similar development in Richmond, see *RE,* 16 Jan. 1855.

·· Chapter Four ··

1. François Alexandre-Frederic, duc de La Rochefoucauld-Liancourt, *Travels through the United States of North America,* 3 vols. (London, 1799), 3:78.

2. Committee of Twenty-Four, *Report of the Minority of the Committee of Twenty-Four on the Subject of Gambling in the City of Richmond* (Richmond, 1833), pp. 6, 16.

3. *BA,* 15 Jan. 1867; Julia Cuthbert Pollard, *Richmond's Story* (Richmond, 1954), p. 87; Dizikes, *Sportsmen and Gamesmen,* pp. 193–214, 307–8.

4. Baily, *Journal of a Tour,* p. 101. For advertisements of cockfights, see *NPH,* 2 Apr. 1803, 20 Mar. 1811. See also Mordecai, *Virginia, Especially Richmond, in By-Gone Days,* p. 263.

5. Jennie Holliman, *American Sports (1785–1835)* (Durham, N.C., 1931), pp. 125, 132; Pickering, *Inquiries of an Emigrant,* pp. 23–24.

6. May, "Dramatic Encyclopedia," reel 1, B6-1804.

7. Pickering, *Inquiries of an Emigrant,* p. 27.

8. John O'Connor, *Wanderings of a Vagabond: An Autobiography,* ed. John Morris (pseud.) (New York, 1873), pp. 229–31, 354; *White Sulphur Papers,* no. 1 (White Sulphur Springs, 1932), p. 6; Herbert Manchester, *Four Centuries of Sport in America, 1490–1890* (New York, 1931), p. 136; Murray, *Lands of the Slave and the Free,* p. 221. For the role of the professional gambler in urban areas, see David R. Johnson, *Policing the Urban Underworld: The Impact of Crime on the Development of the American Police, 1800–1887* (Philadelphia, 1979), p. 7.

9. *American Turf Register* 6 (Dec. 1834); John Hervey, *Racing in America, 1665–1865* (New York, 1944), pp. 11, 19; Beirne, *The Amiable Baltimoreans,* p. 251; *NPH,* 15 Apr. 1811; Charles Stewart, "My Life as a Slave," *Harper's Magazine* 59 (1884): 732; John Rickards Betts, *America's Sporting Heritage, 1850–1950* (Reading, Mass., 1974), p. 41; O'Connor, *Wanderings,* p. 121; *RE,* 18 Aug. 1835.

10. See Richard Ten Broeck to Col. William R. Johnson, 29 July 1844, Henry Clay to Col. Johnson, 8 Feb. 1845, E. M. Blackburn to Col. Johnson, 11 Nov. 1849, Pegram-Johnson-McIntosh Papers, Va. Hist. Soc. See also Littleton Waller Taze-

well Wickham to Elizabeth Selden Maclurg Wickham, 26 Apr. 1838, Wickham Letters, Valentine Museum.

11. Mrs. Anne Ritson, *A Poetical Picture of America, Being of Observations Made, during a Residence of Several Years, at Alexandria, and Norfolk, in Virginia* (London, 1809), p. 80.

12. Mordecai, *Virginia, Especially Richmond, in By-Gone Days,* p. 20; *American Turf Register* 8 (May 1837): 421, 423; Hervey, *Racing in America,* pp. 13, 15; John Bernard, *Retrospections of America, 1797–1811* (New York, 1887), pp. 153–54; *RE,* 3 Sept. 1813. See also *RE,* 3 May 1805; *BA,* 15 July 1813. See *RDC,* 8 May 1813, for a list of owners riding horses in a race.

13. Holliman, *American Sports,* p. 114.

14. *RE,* 15 Apr. 1813; Pickering, *Inquiries of an Emigrant,* p. 35.

15. See *NPH,* 3 Oct. 1831. For the Maryland Jockey Club's rules, see Henry William Herbert, *Frank Forester's Horse and Horsemanship of the United States and British Provinces of North America,* 2 vols. (New York, 1857), 2:525–30. Also see Norfolk Jockey Club, Records, 1826–33, Va. Hist. Soc.; Richmond Jockey Club Minutes, 1824–38 (microfilm), UVA Lib.; Howard, *The Monumental City,* p. 79.

16. Mordecai, *Virginia, Especially Richmond, in By-Gone Days,* p. 252.

17. Forrest, *Historical and Descriptive Sketches,* p. 113. See also La Rochefoucauld-Liancourt, *Travels,* 3:78.

18. Arthur Meier Schlesinger, *The Rise of the City, 1878–1898* (New York, 1933), p. 309.

19. Somers, *The Rise of Sport in New Orleans,* p. 25.

20. *Code of Virginia,* Chapter 147, sec. 1, 4, 5, 7, 17 (1819).

21. Ibid., Chapter 220, sec. 2, 4 (1828).

22. Committee of Twenty-four, *Report of the Committee of Twenty-four Appointed at a Meeting of the Citizens of Richmond, Held the 28th Day of October, 1833, for the Purpose of Devising Means to Suppress the Vice of Gambling in This City* (Richmond, 1833), p. 18.

23. Ibid., pp. 11–12, 17, 22.

24. *Code of Virginia,* Chapter 198, sec. 1, 2, 4 (1849).

25. Ibid., Chapter 198, sec. 5, 6 (1860).

26. *Code of Maryland,* Chapter 110, sec. 1 (1797), Chapter 88, sec. 1 (1826).

27. Ibid., Chapter 190, sec. 1, 3 (1842), Chapter 265, sec. 1, 2 (1853). See also ibid., Chapter 55, sec. 3 (1830), Chapter 136, sec. 1 (1839), Chapter 195, sec. 6 (1856).

28. "Report of the Committee of Finance on Lotteries," *Journal of the House of Delegates of Virginia,* 1825, Appendix.

29. Maryland Constitution (ratified 4 June 1851), art. III, sec. 37; *Code of Virginia,* Chapter 198, sec. 12 (1860).

30. Thomas Ewbank, *Life in Brazil; or, A Journal of a Visit to the Land of the Cocoa and the Palm* (New York, 1856), p. 20.

31. Hess to Mrs. Swift Miller, 18 Feb. 1849, Wooster Papers, Southern Historical Collection, UNC Lib.; Maria Shepherd to John Colin, 6 Mar. 1850, John B. Colin Papers, College of William and Mary.

Notes

32. T. H. Breen, "Horses and Gentlemen: The Cultural Significance of Gambling among the Gentry of Virginia," *William and Mary Quarterly*, 3d ser., 34 (Apr. 1977): 248, 257.

33. See ibid., p. 249.

34. Ibid., p. 257.

35. O'Connor, *Wanderings*, pp. 112, 348.

36. John Boles, *The Great Revival, 1787–1805* (Lexington, Ky., 1972), pp. 193–96.

37. Anne Firor Scott, *The Southern Lady: From Pedestal to Politics, 1830–1930* (Chicago and London, 1970), p. 100.

38. Betts, *America's Sporting Heritage*, p. 17.

39. Ibid.; *Spirit of the Times* 21 (Apr. 5, 1851): 78.

40. Raymond A. Mohl, "Poverty, Pauperism, and Social Order in the Preindustrial American City, 1780–1840," *Social Science Quarterly* 52 (Mar. 1972): 940.

41. Sutton, "Nostalgia, Pessimism, and Malaise," 47, 49, 53.

42. *RE*, 2 Dec. 1853. For examples of arrests, see *BA*, 1 Oct. 1851, 16 July 1855, 1 June 1857, 15 July, 15 Nov. 1867, 1 Sept. 1869; *RW*, 12 Nov. 1867.

43. O'Connor, *Wanderings*, p. 189.

44. Putnam, *Richmond during the War*, pp. 255–56.

45. H. A. Tutwiler to Netta Tutwiler, 3 Apr. 1863, Mrs. Thomas C. McCorvey Papers, Southern Historical Collection, UNC Lib.

46. *RE*, 15 May 1855.

47. Howard, *The Monumental City*, pp. 79–80. See also Francis F. Beirne, *Baltimore . . . A Picture History, 1858–1958* (New York, 1957), p. 44.

48. Herbert, *Frank Forester's Horse and Horsemanship*, 2:126–27.

49. Crane, *Popular Amusements*, p. 64. See also Burton, *History of Norfolk*, p. 18.

·•· **Chapter Five** ·•·

1. Hewitt, *Shadows on the Wall*, pp. 161, 166.

2. See E. Digby Baltzell, *Philadelphia Gentlemen* (Glencoe, Ill., 1958) and *The Protestant Establishment: Aristocracy and Caste in America* (New York, 1964); William H. and Jane H. Pease, *The Web of Progress: Private Values and Public Styles in Boston and Charleston, 1828–1843* (New York, 1985).

3. Owens, *Baltimore on the Chesapeake*, p. 219; Scharf, *History of Baltimore City and County*, 2:765.

4. See *NPH*, 1 Oct. 1803.

5. Memorial Foundation for Children, Records, TS, Va. State Lib.; Kate Cabell Cox, *Historical Sketch of Richmond's Oldest Chartered Charity Memorial Home for Girls* (Richmond, 1925), pp. 7–9; Thomas J. Bagby Papers, Va. State Lib. Suzanne Lebsock notes that in antebellum Petersburg, Virginia, men were not active in charity until the 1850s, when they usurped women's causes, often throwing women into the background in auxiliary organizations (*The Free Women of Petersburg: Status and Culture in a Southern Town, 1784–1860* [New York, 1984], pp. 195–236). I did not find that to be the case in Richmond, where men were active in benevolence even in the eighteenth century. Likewise, some women continued

to play leading roles in benevolent associations, such as the Ladies Aid Association; and they also controlled some civic improvement associations, such as the Hollywood Memorial Association of the Ladies of Richmond. Similarly, women in Norfolk continued their work through such organizations as the Washington and Lee Association, which provided relief to widows and children of Civil War soldiers. See Chesnut, *A Diary from Dixie,* pp. 107–8; Mary H. Mitchell, *Hollywood Cemetery: The History of a Southern Shrine* (Richmond, 1985), pp. 64–66; Burton, *History of Norfolk,* p. 125; *NV,* 15 Dec. 1869.

6. Mordecai, *Virginia, Especially Richmond, in By-Gone Days,* pp. 255–62; Dabney, *Richmond,* p. 69; *American Turf Register* 1 (Sept. 1829): 41; Little, *Richmond,* pp. 205–6; Edmund Berkeley, "Quoits, the Sport of Gentlemen," *Virginia Cavalcade* 15 (Summer 1965): 12, 14–16, 21.

7. Lebsock, *The Free Women,* pp. 215–20.

8. Howard, *The Monumental City,* p. 42.

9. Hewitt, *Shadows on the Wall,* p. 127; Burton, *History of Norfolk,* p. 169; *RE,* 2 Mar. 1809, 23 Feb. 1810; Tyler-McGraw and Kimball, *In Bondage and Freedom,* p. 16.

10. Scharf, *History of Baltimore City and County,* 1:243; Murray, *Lands of the Slave and the Free,* p. 201; Little, *Richmond,* p. 232.

11. Frey, *Reminiscences,* pp. 59, 89; Meredith Janvier, *Baltimore Yesterdays* (Baltimore, 1937), p. 10; Scharf, *History of Baltimore City and County,* 1:243.

12. Murray, *Lands of the Slave and the Free,* p. 222.

13. Quoted in Olson, *Baltimore,* p. 101.

14. Quoted, ibid., p. 119.

15. Murray, *Lands of the Slave and the Free,* pp. 453–55; Howard, *The Monumental City,* p. 83.

16. Vexler, *Baltimore,* pp. 33, 35; Little, *Richmond,* pp. 213, 230–31; Norvell, *Richmond,* n.p.; Christian, *Richmond,* p. 308; Scharf, *History of Baltimore City and County,* 2:757–62; Burton, *History of Norfolk,* pp. 98, 139.

17. [Lucian Minor], "The Temperance Reformation in Virginia," *Southern Literary Messenger* 16 (1850): 427; Jeremiah Bell Jeter, *Recollections of a Long Life* (Richmond, 1891), p. 35; C. C. Pearson and J. Edwin Hendricks, *Liquor and Anti-Liquor in Virginia, 1619–1919* (Durham, N.C., 1967), pp. 55, 59–60; Elizabeth Virginia Lindsay Lomax, Diary, 1 May 1848, Va. Hist. Soc.

18. [Minor], "The Temperance Reformation," p. 430; Pearson and Hendricks, *Liquor and Anti-Liquor,* pp. 33, 49, 63, 74.

19. [Minor], "The Temperance Reformation," pp. 428, 430–31.

20. Quoted in Pearson and Hendricks, *Liquor and Anti-Liquor,* p. 62n.

21. Jeremiah Bell Jeter, *A Memoir of Abner W. Clopton, A.M.* (Richmond, 1837), p. 189.

22. [Minor], "The Temperance Reformation," p. 433; Pearson and Hendricks, *Liquor and Anti-Liquor,* pp. 67, 91, 93.

23. Pearson and Hendricks, *Liquor and Anti-Liquor,* p. 94; John Allen Krout, *The Origins of Prohibition* (New York, 1925), pp. 184, 201–2.

Notes

24. Lorenzo Dow Johnson, *Martha Washingtonianism; or, A History of the Ladies' Temperance Benevolent Societies* (New York, 1843), pp. 22–24.

25. Jill Siegel Dodd, "The Working Classes and the Temperance Movement in Ante-Bellum Boston," *Labor History* 19 (Fall 1978): 511, 523.

26. Olson, *Baltimore*, p. 181.

27. Pearson and Hendricks, *Liquor and Anti-Liquor*, pp. 97–99, 102n.

28. Philip S. White and Ezra S. Ely, "Vindication," quoted in Krout, *Origins of Prohibition*, p. 213.

29. Krout, *Origins of Prohibition*, p. 212.

30. Vexler, *Baltimore*, p. 32; Leroy Graham, *Baltimore: The Nineteenth Century Black Capital* (Lanham, Md., 1982), pp. 133–41; O'Brien, "Factory, Church, and Community," pp. 509–36; Tyler-McGraw and Kimball, *In Bondage and Freedom*, pp. 40–41; Tommy Lee Bogger, "The Slave and Free Black Community in Norfolk, 1775–1865" (Ph.D. diss., University of Virginia, 1976), pp. 310–12. It should not be a surprise that the white citizens saw the black organizations as a threat; see William H. Richardson to the Governor, 12 July 1866, *Calendar of Virginia State Papers*, 11:467. See also *RE*, 4 Jan. 1867.

31. Myron Berman, *Richmond's Jewry, 1769–1976: Shabbat in Shockoe* (Charlottesville, Va., 1979), p. 84; Beirne, *The Amiable Baltimoreans*, pp. 211, 213, 219.

32. Kathy Peiss, *Cheap Amusements: Working Women and Amusements in Turn-of-the-Century New York* (Philadelphia, 1986), p. 31.

33. Isaac M. Fein, *The Making of an American Jewish Community: The History of Baltimore Jewry from 1773 to 1920* (Philadelphia, 1971), pp. 131–32.

34. Beirne, *The Amiable Baltimoreans*, pp. 204–5; Lois B. McCauley, *Maryland Historical Prints, 1752 to 1889: A Selection from the Robert G. Merrick Collection, Maryland Historical Society, and Other Maryland Collections* (Baltimore, 1975), p. 120.

35. *BA*, 22 Aug. 1865, quoted in Olson, *Baltimore*, p. 180.

36. Olson, *Baltimore*, p. 83; Fein, *The Making of an American Jewish Community*, p. 133.

37. Pollard, *Richmond's Story*, p. 177; Edward M. Alfriend, "Social Life in Richmond during the War," *Cosmopolitan* 11 (Dec. 1891): 229; Chesnut, *A Diary from Dixie*, p. 260; Putnam, *Richmond during the War*, p. 270.

38. May, "Dramatic Encyclopedia," reel 7, Li-1860, Ly5-1869; Beirne, *The Amiable Baltimoreans*, pp. 30–31.

39. "Home Club Regulations," Broadside, Gooch Family Papers, Va. Hist. Soc.; Little, *Richmond*, p. 206; *RE*, 4 Jan. 1867; Harry Heth, "Memoirs," TS, Heth-Selden Papers, UVA Lib.; Christian, *Richmond*, p. 367.

40. Henry Clarkson Meredith, *A History of the Norfolk German Club, 1868–1960* ([Norfolk?], 1961), pp. 12–15; Burton, *History of Norfolk*, pp. 180, 183.

41. *NV*, 16 Apr. 1869. See also Holliman, *American Sports*, pp. 156, 159; Burton, *History of Norfolk*, pp. 143, 149, 151.

42. Hardy, *How Boston Played*, pp. 129, 139, 146.

Notes

43. Benjamin G. Rader, *American Sports: From the Age of Folk Games to the Age of Spectators* (Englewood Cliffs, N.J., 1983), p. 52.

·•· **Chapter Six** ·•·

1. Janson, *The Stranger in America,* p. 305.
2. *RE,* 17 Dec. 1807.
3. See *NPH,* 14 Apr. 1803; Mordecai, *Virginia, Especially Richmond, in By-Gone Days,* pp. 217, 219; Sally E. Hollingsworth to Miss Ruth Tobin, 10 May 1811, Hollingsworth Letters, TS, Md. Hist. Soc.
4. Scharf, *History of Baltimore City and County,* 2:678. See also Hewitt, *Shadows on the Wall,* pp. 115–19.
5. Paton Yoder, "The American Inn, 1775–1850: Melting Pot or Stewing Kettle?" *Indiana Magazine of History* 59 (1963): 151.
6. *RE,* 1 Mar. 1811; *RDC,* 1 May 1813, 21 Mar. 1817; *NPH,* 16 June 1819, 15 June 1827; Mordecai, *Virginia, Especially Richmond, in By-Gone Days,* p. 220.
7. See Lydia E. Hollingsworth to Ruth Tobin, 8 Apr. 1811, Hollingsworth Letters, TS, Md. Hist. Soc.; Samuel G. Adams to Col. Richard Adams, 10 Feb. 1813, Adams Family Papers, College of William and Mary; G. N. Johnson to Marguerite Johnson, 8 Jan. 1837, George Nicholson Johnson Papers, Va. Hist. Soc.; Murray, *Travels in North America,* 1:160; Minnie to Frances Johnson, 2 Feb. 1848, Frances Jane Johnson Caskie Papers, Va. Hist. Soc.
8. *RDC,* 8 June 1813. For dancing in Norfolk, see Ritson, *A Poetical Picture of America,* pp. 98–99.
9. Ellen Wayles Randolph to Martha J. Randolph, [2] Mar., 30 Mar., 24 Apr. 1814, Jefferson Family Correspondence, UVA Lib.
10. Thomas Massie to William Massie, 5 Feb. 1826, Thomas Massie Papers, Va. Hist. Soc. For a funeral invitation, see the Ella Noland Mackensie Papers, Southern Historical Collection, UNC Lib.
11. Godfrey Thomas Vigne, *Six Months in America,* 2 vols. (London, 1832), 1:129–30; Charles Joseph Latrobe, *The Rambler in North America, 1832–1833* (London, 1835), pp. 30–31.
12. Putnam, *Richmond during the War,* p. 345; *RE,* 3 May 1864; Anita Dwyer Withers Diary, 28 Mar. 1864, Southern Historical Collection, UNC Lib.; Chesnut, *A Diary from Dixie,* pp. 268, 273, 282, 284, 287; Sally Grattan to Alexander Brown, 11 Feb. 1862, Alexander Brown Papers, Duke Univ.; Kate Mason Rowland Diary, Confederate Museum, Richmond, quoted in Katherine M. Jones, *Ladies of Richmond, Confederate Capital* (Indianapolis, 1962), p. 148.
13. Judith Brockenbrough McGuire, *Diary of a Southern Refugee, during the War,* 2d ed. (New York, 1868), p. 96; Phoebe Y. Pember to Mrs. Gilmer, 30 Dec. 1863, Phoebe Y. Pember Letters, Southern Historical Collection, UNC Lib.; Mary Newton Stanard, *Richmond: Its People and Its Story* (Philadelphia, 1923), p. 176; Mrs. Roger A. Pryor, *Reminiscences of Peace and War,* rev. ed. (New York, 1924), pp. 263–64; Anita Dwyer Withers Diary, 10 Feb. 1863, Southern Historical Collection, UNC Lib.
14. *RE,* 18 June, 16 July 1811, 17 June 1815, 1 July 1823; Chapman Johnson to

Notes

George Nicholson Johnson, 26 Aug. 1826, George Nicholson Johnson Papers, Va. Hist. Soc.; *BA*, 15 Aug. 1811, 1 July 1823.

15. James Kirke Paulding, *Letters from the South*, 2 vols. (New York, 1817), 1:231–32.

16. *RE*, 2 July 1813.

17. *NPH*, 1 July 1829; *BA*, 15 June 1825; *RE*, 1 July 1823.

18. *RE*, 2 July 1830; Featherstonhaugh, *Excursion through the Slave States*, p. 12.

19. *RE*, 1 July 1845. For advertisements during the last quarter of the century, see the *NV* for the summer of 1879.

20. John W. M. Williams Diary, Summer 1857, John W. M. Williams Papers, Southern Historical Collection, UNC Lib.

21. William Maxwell to Louisa Maxwell Holmes, 2 Sept. 1813, Cocke Family Papers, UVA Lib.; John Campbell to Claiborne W. Gooch, 28 Aug. 1814, Gooch Family Papers, Va. Hist. Soc.; *RE*, 2 Nov. 1855, 2 Aug. 1859; *BA*, 1 Aug. 1843.

22. Philip Holbrook Nicklin, *Letters Descriptive of the Virginia Springs* (Philadelphia, 1835), pp. 29–30; Perceval Reniers, *The Springs of Virginia* (Chapel Hill, N.C., 1941), p. 41. See also Wickham Letters, Valentine Museum. Although Francis Walker Gilmer initially visited the springs for health reasons, in the 1820s his visits became "almost purely social and recreational" (Richard Beale Davis, *Francis Walker Gilmer: Life and Learning in Jefferson's Virginia* [Richmond, 1939], pp. 151–57).

23. *BA*, 1 Aug. 1851; [Edward C. Bruce], "Loungings in the Footprints of the Pioneers," *Harper's New Monthly Magazine* 20 (May 1860): 728–29.

24. Mark Pencil [pseud.], *The White Sulphur Papers* (New York, 1839), p. 27; Little, *Richmond*, p. 225; Reniers, *The Springs*, p. 41; *RE*, 4 July 1843.

25. *BA*, 15 July 1829.

26. John Campbell to Claiborne W. Gooch, 3 Aug. [1814], Gooch Family Papers, Va. Hist. Soc.; John P. MacKensie to Ella Noland MacKensie, 20 Aug. 1856, Ella Noland MacKensie Papers, Southern Historical Collection, UNC Lib.; Littleton Waller Tazewell Wickham to Elizabeth Selden Maclurg Wickham, 21 Aug. 1847, Wickham Letters, Valentine Museum.

27. Pauline to Cornelia Storrs, 20 Aug. 1836, 27 Aug. 1838, Cornelia Storrs Paper, Duke Univ.

28. Boling Hubard to Philip A. Hubard, 1 Sept. 1872, Hubard Family Papers, UVA Lib.; McGuire, *Diary*, pp. 88, 115.

29. Nicklin, *Letters*, pp. 24–25, 29–30.

30. Captain Frederick Marryat, *A Diary in America, with Remarks on Its Institutions* (Philadephia, 1839), quoted in Allan Nevins, ed., *America through British Eyes*, new ed. (Gloucester, Mass., 1968), p. 177. See also Featherstonhaugh, *Excursion through the Slave States*, pp. 21–29.

31. Bina to Cousin Mary, 17 Aug. [during war], Frank Noland Papers, UVA Lib.; Anita Dwyer Withers Diary, 2 Aug. 1862, Southern Historical Collection, UNC Lib.; David Stick, *The Outer Banks of North Carolina* (Chapel Hill, 1958), p. 106. For wartime advertisements, see *RE*, summer of 1863.

Notes

32. These photographs are in the vertical files of the Valentine Museum.

33. *BA,* various issues, 1850; Stanley Lebergott, *Manpower in Economic Growth: An American Record since 1800* (New York, 1964), p. 541. Lebergott (pp. 329–31, 333) indicates that for the same time the annual salary for ministers was $400 and for physicians, $1,000.

34. *BA,* 1 Oct. 1845.

35. Christiana Lippincott to Anne C. Coleman, 1 Apr. 1833, Anne Caroline Coleman Papers, Md. Hist. Soc.

36. Freidrich Ludwig Georg von Raumer, *America and the American People* (New York, 1846), p. 492; Shockley, "A History of the Theatre," p. 52n; Burton, *History of Norfolk,* p. 25.

37. Reuel Denney, *The Astonished Muse* (Chicago, 1957), p. 13.

38. Thorstein Veblen, *The Theory of the Leisure Class* (New York, 1899), p. 86.

39. John Neulinger and Miranda Breit, "Attitude Dimensions of Leisure," *Journal of Leisure Research* 1 (1969): 256.

·· **Conclusion** ··

1. May, "Dramatic Encyclopedia," reel 1, B3-1803.

2. *NV,* 1 Apr. 1867.

3. David R. Goldfield, "Disease and Urban Image: Yellow Fever in Norfolk, 1855," *Virginia Cavalcade* 23 (Autumn 1973): 40.

4. Berlin, *Slaves without Masters,* and Wade, *Slavery in the Cities.*

5. See Scharf, *History of Baltimore City and County,* 2:603.

6. *BA,* 1 Mar., 15 Apr. 1859.

Notes

Select Bibliography

Manuscripts

William R. Perkins Library, Duke University
    Alexander Brown Papers
    Campbell Family Papers
    Mary Brand Dall Correspondence
    Sallie M. H. Fulton Papers
    George Wesley Johnson Papers
    McMullen Family Papers
    Munford-Ellis Papers
    Anna Maria Smith Papers
    Anne P. Smith Papers
    Cornelia Storrs Papers

Maryland Historical Society
    Elizabeth Patterson Bonaparte Papers
    Anne Caroline Coleman Papers
    Grundy-Gibson Papers
    Samuel Hoffman Papers
    Hollingsworth Letters
    Alonzo May Papers
    Sarah Cushing Morris Papers
    Martha Elizabeth Harris Harris Diary
    Louisa G. Mason Diary

Southern Historical Collection, University of North Carolina Library, Chapel Hill
    Hope Bain Papers
    Charles W. Dabney Papers and Books
    John Beauchamp Jones Papers
    Ella Noland Mackensie Papers
    Mrs. Thomas C. McCorvey Papers
    Phoebe Y. Pember Letters
    Daniel A. Penick Papers
    James Ryder Randall Papers
    Anne Gales Root Papers

Starke, Marchant, and Martin Family Papers
John W. M. Williams Papers
Norvell Winsboro Wilson Papers
Anita Dwyer Withers Diary, 1860–65
Wooster Papers
Benjamin C. Yancey letter, 8 Jan. 1865
Valentine Museum
    Edwin V. Valentine, "Notes on Nineteenth-Century Amusements"
    Vertical Files
    Wickham Letters
University of Virginia Library
    Cocke Family Papers
    Duval Family Papers
    Heth-Selden Papers
    Hubard Family Papers
    Jefferson Family Correspondence
    Frank Noland Papers
    Norfolk Female Orphan Society Record Books, 1816–1949
    Norfolk Jockey Club Book, 1826–33
    Oliver Family Papers
    Richmond Jockey Club Minutes, 1824–38
    Augustus B. Sage letter, 20 Dec. 1862
    Martin Baskett Shepherd Papers
    Webb-Prentis Papers
Virginia Historical Society
    George William Bagby Papers
    Thomas Bolling Scrapbook
    Frances Jean Johnson Caskie Papers
    Couper Family Papers
    Daniel Family Correspondence
    Dearing Family Papers
    Gooch Family Papers
    Hugh Blair Grigsby Diary and Letters
    George E. Harrison Letters
    Lancaster Family Papers
    Elizabeth Virginia Lindsay Lomax Diaries, 17 Mar. 1848–31 Jan. 1863
    George Nicholson Johnson Papers
    Thomas Massie Papers
    "Music and the Theatre" (typed manuscript)
    Norfolk Jockey Club, Records, 1826–33
    Pegram-Johnson-McIntosh Family Papers

Select Bibliography

Mary Jefferson Randolph Commonplace Book

John Coles Rutherfoord Diary

Rutherford Family Papers

Frances Amanda Booth Taliaferro Papers

Andrew Talcott Diary, 1 Jan. 1840–15 July 1840

Thomas Family Papers

Westmoreland Club Records, 1877–1942

Williams Family Papers

Virginia State Library, Archives Section

    Thomas J. Bagby Papers

    Memorial Foundation for Children Records

Earl Gregg Swem Library, College of William and Mary

    Adams Family Papers

    Gideon Christian Papers

    John B. Colin Papers

    James Barron Hope Papers

    Levin Joynes Papers

    Tucker-Coleman Collection

Jerry Showalter (private collection), Ivy, Virginia

    John J. Moorman, "My Mother. A Memento of the Life, and Character, of Mrs. Martha Jane Moorman: Together with a part of her Correspondence. Compiled for the use of her Children." Harrisonburg, 20 May 1835.

Documents

Baltimore Criminal Justice Commission. *Report on Legalized Gambling.* Baltimore, [1964].

Boyd's Directory of Richmond City and a Business Directory of Norfolk, Lynchburg, Petersburg, and Richmond, 1870. Richmond: Bates & Waddy Brothers, 1870.

The City of Richmond Business Directory and City Guide. Richmond: Mills and Starke, 1866.

Committee of Twenty-four. *Report of the Committee of Twenty-four Appointed at a Meeting of the Citizens of Richmond Held the 28th Day of October, 1833, For the Purpose of Devising Means to Suppress the Vice of Gambling in this City.* Richmond, 1833.

———. *Report of the Minority of the Committee of Twenty-four on the Subject of Gambling in the City of Richmond.* Richmond, 1833.

Maryland. *Laws of Maryland.* Annapolis, 1799.

———. *Laws of Maryland.* Annapolis, 1827.

———. *Laws of Maryland.* Annapolis, 1830.

———. *Laws of Maryland.* Annapolis, 1831.

———. *Laws of Maryland.* Annapolis, 1843.

———. *Laws of Maryland.* Annapolis, 1853.

———. *Laws of Maryland*. Annapolis, 1856.

Montague's Richmond Directory and Business Advertiser for 1850. Richmond: W. L. Montague, 1850.

Richmond City Directory Containing a General Directory of the Citizens of Richmond and Manchester, and also a Business Directory, 1873–4. Richmond: B. W. Gillis, 1873.

The Richmond Directory and Business Advertiser, for 1856. Richmond: Ellyson's Steam Presses, 1856.

The Richmond Directory, Register, and Almanac, for the Year 1819. Richmond: J. Maddox, 1819.

Sheriff & Co.'s Richmond City Directory, 1876–7. Richmond: Sheriff & Co., 1876.

United States. *Aggregate Amount of Each Description of Persons within the United States of America and Territories Thereof, Agreeably to Actual Enumeration Made according to Law*. Washington, D.C.: [n.p.], 1811.

———. *Census for 1820*. Washington, D.C.: Gales & Seaton, 1821.

———. *Fifth Census, or Enumeration of the Inhabitants of the United States, 1830*. Washington, D.C.: Duff Green, 1832.

———. *Report of the Whole Number of Persons within the Several Districts of the United States. According to "An Act Providing for the Second Census or Enumeration of the Inhabitants of the United States."* Washington, D.C.: Duane, 1801.

———. *The Seventh Census of the United States: 1850*. Washington, D.C.: Robert Armstrong, 1853.

———. *Sixth Census, or Enumeration of the Inhabitants of the United States as Corrected at the Department of State in 1840*. Washington, D.C.: Blair and Rives, 1841.

———. *The Statistics of the Population of the United States, Embracing the Tables of Race, Nationality, Sex, Selected Ages, and Occupations*. Washington, D.C.: Government Printing Office, 1872.

———. *Statistics of the United States, (including Mortality, Property, &c.) in 1860; Compiled from the Original Returns and Being the Final Exhibit of the Eighth Census*. Washington, D.C.: Government Printing Office, 1866.

Virginia. *Calendar of Virginia State Papers*, vol. 11. Richmond, 1876.

———. *Code of Virginia*. Richmond, 1819.

———. *Code of Virginia, Supplement*. Richmond, 1833.

———. *Code of Virginia*. Richmond, 1849.

———. "Report of the Committee of Finance on Lotteries." *Journal of the House of Delegates of Virginia*, 1825, Appendix.

Newspapers

Baltimore American and Commercial Daily Advertiser, 1801–69. (Known variously as the *American and Mercantile Daily Advertiser*, the *American and Commercial Daily Advertiser*, the *American and Commercial Advertiser*, and the *Baltimore American and Commercial Daily Advertiser*.)

Norfolk and Portsmouth Herald, 1801–59. (Known variously as the *Norfolk & Portsmouth Herald and General Advertiser*, the *Norfolk & Portsmouth Herald and Daily Commercial Advertiser*, and the *Norfolk & Portsmouth Herald.*)

Norfolk Virginian, 1865–79.

Richmond Daily Compiler, miscellaneous issues.

Richmond Enquirer, 1801–77. (Known variously as the *Daily Richmond Enquirer*, the *Weekly Richmond Enquirer*, the *Daily Enquirer and Examiner*, and the *Richmond Enquirer.*)

Richmond Whig, 1835–61. (Known variously as *the Constitutional Whig*, the *Daily Richmond Whig*, the *Richmond Whig and Public Advertiser*, the *Richmond Whig and Commercial Journal*, the *Daily Richmond Whig and Public Advertiser*, the *Weekly Whig*, the *Richmond Whig and Advertiser*, the *Daily Richmond Whig*, and the *Richmond Daily Whig.*)

Writings of Contemporaries

Akers, Bryan, ed. *Graphic Description of the Burning of the Richmond Theatre, December 26, 1811.* Lynchburg, Va.: News Book and Job Office Print., 1879.

Alexander, Archibald. *A Discourse Occasioned by the Burning of the Theatre in the City of Richmond, Va., on the Twenty-Sixth of December, 1811.* Philadelphia: John Weldwood Scott, 1812.

Alfriend, Edward M. "Social Life in Richmond during the War." *Cosmopolitan* 11 (Dec. 1891): 229–33.

[Andrews, Charles Wesley.] *On the Incompatibility of Theater-Going and Dancing with Membership in the Christian Church. An Address of the Convocation of the Valley of Virginia, to the People of Their Respective Parishes.* Philadelphia: Office of Leighton Publications, 1872.

Arese, Count Francesco. *A Trip to the Prairies and in the Interior of North America, 1837–1838.* Trans. Andrew Evans. New York: Harbor Press, 1934.

Audubon, John James. *Letters of John James Audubon.* 2 vols. Boston: Club of Odd Volumes, 1930.

Baily, Francis. *Journal of a Tour in Unsettled Parts of North America, in 1796 and 1797.* London: Baily Bros., 1856.

Barnum, Phineas Taylor. *Struggles and Triumphs; or, Forty Years' Recollections of P. T. Barnum.* Rept. New York: Macmillan Co., 1930.

Bernard, John. *Retrospections of America, 1797–1811.* New York: Harper & Brothers, 1887.

Bethune, George W. *Sermons.* Philadelphia: Mentz & Rovoudt, 1846.

Birkbeck, Morris. *Notes on a Journey in America.* 3d. ed. London: Severn & Co., for J. Ridgway, 1819.

Bowen, Eli. *Rambles in the Path of the Steam-Horse.* Philadelphia: W. Bromwell & W. W. Smith, 1855.

Brackenridge, Henry M. *Recollections of Persons and Places in the West*. Philadelphia: J. Kay, jun. & brother, 1834.

[Bruce, Edward C.] "Loungings in the Footprints of the Pioneers." *Harper's New Monthly Magazine* 20 (May 1860): 721–36.

Buckingham, James Silk. *America, Historical, Statistic, and Descriptive*. 2 vols. New York: Harper & Brothers, 1841.

By a Member of the Society [John Zug]. *The Foundation, Progress, and Principles of the Washington Temperance Society of Baltimore, and the Influence It Has Had on the Temperance Movements in the United States*. Baltimore: J. D. Toy, 1842.

Calamity at Richmond. Philadelphia: John F. Watson, 1812.

Chesnut, Mary Boykin. *A Diary from Dixie*. Ed. Isabella D. Martin and Myrta Lockett Avary. Rept. Gloucester, Mass.: Peter Smith, 1961.

Chesterman, William Dallas. *Guide to Richmond and the Battle-Fields*. Richmond: J. E. Goode, 1881.

Chevalier, Michel. *Society, Manners, and Politics in the United States: Letters on North America*. New ed. Ed. John William Ward. Ithaca, N.Y.: Cornell University Press, 1969.

Chickering, Rev. John W. "The Reciprocal Influence of Piety and Taste," *Christian Keepsake and Missionary Annual* (1839): 71–77.

Clark, Martha. *Victims of Amusements*. Philadelphia: T. B. Peterson, 1849.

Coke, Edward T. *A Subaltern's Furlough: Descriptive of Scenes in Various Parts of the United States, Upper and Lower Canada*. London: Saunders & Otley, 1833.

Corning, James Leonard. *The Christian Law of Amusement*. Buffalo: Phinney & Company, 1859.

Crane, Rev. J. T. *Popular Amusements*. Cincinnati: Hitchcock & Walden, 1869.

Cuyler, T. L. *Sermon on Christian Recreation and Unchristian Amusement*. New York: Barker, 1858.

Davidge, William. *Footlight Flashes*. New York: American News Company, 1866.

Davis, Stephen. *Notes of a Tour in America, in 1832 and 1833*. Edinburgh: Waugh & Innes, 1833.

Dix, John Ross. *Transatlantic Tracings; or, Sketches of Persons and Scenes in America*. London: W. Tweedie, 1853.

Duncan, John M. *Travels through Part of the United States and Canada in 1818 and 1819*. New York: W. B. Gilley, 1823.

Dunlap, William. *A History of the American Theatre*. New York: J. & J. Harper, 1832.

Ewbank, Thomas. *Life in Brazil; or, A Journal of a Visit to the Land of the Cocoa and the Palm*. New York: Harper & Brothers, 1856.

Fearon, Henry Bradshaw. *Sketches of America*. London: Longman, Hurst, Rees, Orme and Brown, 1818.

Featherstonhaugh, George William. *Excursion through the Slave States*. New York: Harper and Brothers, 1844.

Forrest, William S. *Historical and Descriptive Sketches of Norfolk and Vicinity.* Philadelphia: Lindsay & Blakiston, 1853.

Frey, Jacob. *Reminiscences of Baltimore.* Baltimore: Maryland Book Concern, 1893.

Full Account of the Burning of the Richmond Theatre. Richmond: J. E. Goode, 1858.

Gilder, R. W. "Certain Tendencies in Current Literature." *New Princeton Review* 4 (1887): 1–13.

Griffith, Thomas Waters. *Annals of Baltimore.* Baltimore: W. Woody, 1824.

Hale, Edward E. *Public Amusement for Poor and Rich: A Discourse Delivered before the Church of the Unity, Worcester, December 16, 1855.* Boston: Phillips, Sampson & Co., 1857.

Hall, Francis. *Travels in Canada, and the United States, in 1816 and 1817.* Boston: Wells and Lilly, 1818.

Hall, Margaret Hunter. *The Aristocratic Journey; Being the Outspoken Letters of Mrs. Basil Hall Written during a Fourteen Months' Sojourn in America, 1827–1828.* Ed. Una Pope-Hennessy. New York: G. P. Putnam's Sons, 1931.

Hamilton, Thomas. *Men and Manners in America.* Edinburgh: William Blackwood, 1833.

Hancock, William. *An Emigrant's Five Years in the Free States of America.* London: T. C. Newby, 1860.

Harris, William Tell. *Remarks Made during a Tour through the United States of America.* London: Sherwood, Neely, & Jones, 1821.

Haussonville, Gabriel Paul Othein de Cleron, comte d'. *A travers les Etats-Unis, notes et impressions (Across the United States, notes and impressions).* Paris: C. Levy, 1883.

[Hawkins, Archibald]. *The Life and Times of Hon. Elijah Stansbury, an "Old Defender" and Ex-Mayor of Baltimore: Together with Early Reminiscences, Dating from 1662, and Embracing a Period of 212 Years.* Baltimore: J. Murphy & Co., 1874.

Haydn, H. C. *Amusements, in the Light of Reason and Scripture.* New York: American Tract Society, 1880.

Henry, Thomas Charlton. *An Inquiry into the Consistency of Popular Amusements with a Profession of Christianity.* Charleston, S.C.: Wm. Riley, 1825.

Herbert, Henry William. *The Complete Manual for Young Sportsmen.* New York: Stringer & Townsend, 1856.

——. *Field Sports in the United States.* 2 vols. London: Richard Bentley, 1848.

——. *Frank Forester's Horse and Horsemanship of the United States and British Provinces of North America.* 2 vols. New York: Stringer & Townsend, 1857.

Hewitt, John H. *Shadows on the Wall; or, Glimpses of the Past.* Baltimore: Turnbull Brothers, 1877.

Hodgson, Adam. *Letters from North America, Written during a tour in the United States and Canada.* 2 vols. London: Hurst, Robinson & Co., 1824.

Houstoun, Mrs. Matilda C. *Hesperos; or, Travels in the West.* 2 vols. London: J. W. Parker, 1850.

Howard, George W. *The Monumental City, Its Past History and Present Resources.* Baltimore: J. D. Ehlers & Co., 1873–76.

Hundley, Daniel R. *Social Relations in Our Southern States.* Ed. William J. Cooper, Jr. New York: H. B. Price, 1860; rept. Baton Rouge: Louisiana State University Press, 1979.

Janson, Charles William. *The Stranger in America: Containing Observations Made during a Long Residence in That Country.* London: J. Cundee, 1807.

Jeter, Jeremiah Bell. *A Memoir of Abner W. Clopton, A.M.* Richmond: Yale & Wyatt, 1837.

———. *Recollections of a Long Life.* Richmond: Religious Herald Co., 1891.

Johnson, Lorenzo Dow. *Martha Washingtonianism; or, A History of the Ladies' Temperance Benevolent Societies.* New York: Saxton & Miles, 1843.

[Johnson, Oliver.] Testimony of Progressive Friends. *Amusements: Their Uses and Abuses.* New York: Johnson, [1856].

Kennedy, John Pendleton. *Address Delivered before the Maryland Institute for the Promotion of the Mechanic Arts, on the Occasion of the Opening of the Fourth Annual Exhibition, on the 21st October, 1851, Being the First Exhibition in the New Hall of the Institute.* Baltimore: J. Murphy & Co., 1851.

———. *At Home and Abroad.* New York: G. P. Putnam & Sons, 1872.

———. *Swallow Barn.* Rev. ed. New York: G. P. Putnam, 1852.

La Rouchefoucauld-Liancourt, François Alexandre-Frederic, duc de. *Travels through the United States of North America.* Vol. 3. London: R. Phillips, 1799.

Latham, Henry. *Black and White, a Journal of a Three Months' Tour in the United States.* London: Macmillan & Co., 1867.

Latrobe, Charles Joseph. *The Rambler in North America, 1832–1833.* London: R. B. Seeley & W. Burnside, 1835.

Latrobe, John H. B. "Reminiscences of Baltimore in 1824." *Maryland Historical Magazine* 1 (June 1906): 113–24.

Little, John P. *Richmond, the Capital of Virginia: Its History.* Richmond: Macfarlane & Fergusson, 1851.

McGuire, Judith Brockenbrough. *Diary of a Southern Refugee, during the War.* 2d ed. New York: E. J. Hale & Son, 1868.

Malet, William Wyndham. *An Errand to the South in the Summer of 1862.* London: R. Bentley, 1863.

Marryat, Captain Frederick. *A Diary in America, with Remarks on Its Institutions.* Philadelphia: Carey & Hart, 1839. Quoted in Allan Nevins, ed. *America through British Eyes.* New ed. Gloucester, Mass.: Peter Smith, 1968, pp. 171–88.

Mattison, Hiram. *Popular Amusements: An Appeal to Methodists.* New York: Carlton & Porter, 1867.

Mendell, Miss. *Notes of Travel and Life.* New York: [n.p.], 1854.

[Minor, Lucian.] "The Temperance Reformation in Virginia." *Southern Literary Messenger* 16 (1850): 426–38.

Mordecai, Samuel. *Virginia, Especially Richmond, in By-Gone Days.* Richmond: West & Johnston, 1860.

Morison, J. H. "Amusements." *Monthly Religious Magazine and Independent Journal* 21 (Jan. 1859): 26–38.

Murray, Sir Charles Augustus. *Travels in North America during the Years 1834, 1835, and 1836.* 2 vols. London: R. Bentley, 1839.

Murray, Henry A. *Lands of the Slave and the Free; or, Cuba, the United States, and Canada.* 2d ed. London: G. Routledge & Co., 1857.

Murray, Hugh. *Historical Account of Discoveries and Travels in North America.* 2 vols. London: Longman, Rees, Orme, Brown & Green, 1829.

Nicklin, Philip Holbrook. *Letters Descriptive of the Virginia Springs.* Philadelphia: H. S. Tanner, 1835.

Norfolk Junior Volunteers. *Byelaws of the Norfolk Junior Volunteers, in the Borough of Norfolk.* Norfolk: J. O'Connor, 1806.

The North American Tourist. New York: A. T. Goodrich, 1839.

O'Connor, John. *Wanderings of a Vagabond. An Autobiography.* Ed. John Morris [pseud.]. New York: John O'Connor, 1873.

Parsons, C. B. *The Pulpit and the Stage; or, The Two Itinerancies. An Historic, Biographic, Philosophic Miscellany.* Nashville: Southern Methodist Publishing House, 1860.

Paulding, James Kirke. *Letters from the South.* 2 vols. New York: James Eastburn & Co., 1817.

Pencil, Mark [pseud.]. *The White Sulphur Papers, or Life at the Springs of Western Virginia.* New York: S. Colman, 1839.

Pickering, Joseph. *Inquiries of an Emigrant: Being the Narrative of an English Farmer from the Year 1824 to 1830.* 3d ed. London: E. Wilson, 1832.

Playfair, Robert. *Recollections of a Visit to the United States and the British Provinces of North America, in the Years 1847, 1848, and 1849.* Edinburgh: T. Constable, 1856.

Power, Tyrone. *Impressions of America during the Years 1833, 1834, and 1835.* 2 vols. London: R. Bentley, 1836.

Priest, William. *Travels in the United States of America.* London: Printed for J. Johnson, 1802.

Pryor, Mrs. Roger A. *Reminiscences of Peace and War.* Rev. ed. New York: Macmillan, 1924.

Putnam, Sallie Ann Brock. *Richmond during the War: Four Years of Personal Observation. By a Richmond Lady.* New York: G. W. Carleton & Co., 1867.

Raumer, Friedrich Ludwig George von. *America and the American People.* New York: J. & H. G. Langley, 1846.

Reed, Andrew. *A Narrative of the Visit to the American Churches.* 2 vols. London: Jackson and Walford, 1835.

"Richmond Alarm." *Publications of the New England Tract Society* 6 (1821): 233–36.

Ritson, Anne. *A Poetical Picture of America, Being of Observations Made, during a Residence of Several Years, at Alexandria, and Norfolk, in Virginia.* London: W. Wilson, 1809.

Royall, Anne Newport. *The Black Book; or, A Continuation of Travels in the United States.* 3 vols. Washington, D.C.: [n.p.], 1828–29.

———. *Mrs. Royall's Southern Tour; or, Second Series of the Black Book.* 3 vols. Washington, D.C.: [n.p.], 1830–31.

Sala, George Augustus. *America Revisited.* Vol. 1. London: Vizetelly, 1883.

Sawyer, Frederic William. *Hits at American Whims and Hints for Home Use.* Boston: Walker, Wise, 1860.

———. *A Plea for Amusements.* New York: D. Appleton and Company, 1847.

Scharf, John Thomas. *The Chronicles of Baltimore.* Baltimore: Turnbull Brothers, 1874.

———. *History of Baltimore City and County.* 2 vols. in 1. Philadelphia: L. H. Everts, 1881. Rev. ed. 2 vols. Baltimore: Regional Publishing Co., 1971.

Smith, Daniel E. Huger, Alice R. Huger Smith, and Arney R. Childs, eds. *Mason Smith Family Letters, 1860–1868.* Columbia: University of South Carolina Press, 1950.

Somers, Robert. *The Southern States since the War, 1870–1.* London: Macmillan and Co., 1871.

Stewart, Charles, "My Life as a Slave." *Harper's Magazine* 59 (1884): 730–38.

Trollope, Frances. *Domestic Manners of the Americans.* 2 vols. London: Whittaker, Treacher & Co., 1832.

Vigne, Godfrey Thomas. *Six Months in America.* 2 vols. London: Whittaker, Treacher & Co., 1832.

Weld, Charles Richard. *A Vacation Tour in the United States and Canada.* London: Longman, Brown, Green, and Longmans, 1855.

Wood, William B. *Personal Recollections of the Stage, Embracing Notices of Actors, Authors, and Auditors.* Philadelphia: H. C. Baird, 1855.

Zincke, F. Barham. *Last Winter in the United States.* London: J. Murray, 1868.

Secondary Sources: Books and Articles

Altick, Richard D. *The Shows of London.* Cambridge, Mass.: Belknap Press, 1978.

Ariès, Philippe. *Centuries of Childhood: A Social History of Family Life.* New York: Alfred A. Knopf, 1962.

Bailey, Peter. *Leisure and Class in Victorian England: Rational Recreation and the Contest for Control, 1830–1885.* London: Routledge & K. Paul, 1978.

Ball, Donald W., and John W. Loy, eds. *Sport and Social Order: Contributions to the Sociology of Sport.* Reading, Mass.: Addison-Wesley, 1975.

Baltzell, E. Digby. *Philadelphia Gentlemen.* Glencoe, Ill.: Free Press, 1958.

——. *The Protestant Establishment: Aristocracy and Caste in America.* New York: Random House, 1964.

Bayley, David H., ed. *Police and Society.* Beverly Hills, Calif., and London: Sage Publications, 1977.

Beirne, Francis F. *The Amiable Baltimoreans.* New York: Dutton, 1951.

——. *Baltimore . . . A Picture History, 1858–1958.* New York: Hastings House, 1957.

Bender, Thomas. *Toward an Urban Vision: Ideas and Institutions in Nineteenth Century America.* Baltimore: John Hopkins University Press, 1982.

Berkeley, Edmund. "Quoits, the Sport of Gentlemen." *Virginia Cavalcade* 15 (Summer 1965): 11–21.

Berlin, Ira. *Slaves without Masters: The Free Negro in the Antebellum South.* New York: Pantheon Press, 1974.

Berman, Myron. *Richmond's Jewry, 1769–1976: Shabbat in Shockoe.* Charlottesville: University Press of Virginia, 1979.

Bernard, Richard M. "A Portrait of Baltimore in 1800: Economic and Occupational Patterns in an Early American City." *Maryland Historical Magazine* 69 (1974): 341–60.

Betts, John Rickards. *America's Sporting Heritage, 1850–1950.* Reading, Mass.: Addison-Wesley, 1974.

——. "P. T. Barnum and the Popularization of Natural History." *Journal of the History of Ideas* 20 (June–September 1959): 353–68.

——. "The Technological Revolution and the Rise of Sport: 1850–1900." *Mississippi Valley Historical Review* 40 (Sept. 1953): 231–56.

Bishir, Catherine W. *The "Unpainted Aristocracy": The Beach Cottages of Old Nags Head.* Raleigh, N.C.: Division of Archives and History, 1978.

Bode, Carl. *The American Lyceum: Town Meeting of the Mind.* New York: Oxford University Press, 1956.

——. *The Anatomy of American Popular Culture, 1840–1861.* Berkeley and Los Angeles: University of California Press, 1959.

Boles, John. *The Great Revival, 1787–1805.* Lexington: University Press of Kentucky, 1972.

Bondurant, Agnes. *Poe's Richmond.* Richmond: Garrett & Massie, 1942.

Breen, T. H. "Horses and Gentlemen: The Cultural Significance of Gambling among the Gentry of Virginia." *William and Mary Quarterly,* 3d ser., 34 (April 1977): 239–57.

Burch, William R. "The Social Circles of Leisure: Competing Explanations." *Journal of Leisure Research* 1 (1969): 125–47.

Burton, H. W. *The History of Norfolk, Virginia: A Review of Important Events and Incidents Which Occurred from 1763 to 1877; Also a Record of Personal Reminiscences and Political, Commercial, and Curious Facts.* Norfolk: Norfolk Virginian Job Print., 1877.

Charlesworth, James C. *Leisure in America: Blessing or Curse?* Philadelphia: American Academy of Political and Social Science, 1964.

Chesson, Michael B. *Richmond after the War, 1865–1890.* Richmond: Virginia State Library, 1981.

Christian, W. Asbury. *Richmond, Her Past and Present.* Richmond: L. H. Jenkins, 1912.

Clarke, Alfred C. "The Use of Leisure and Its Relation to Levels of Occupational Prestige." *American Sociological Review* 21 (June 1956): 301–7.

Cole, Arthur Charles. *The Irrepressible Conflict, 1850–1865.* New York: Macmillan Co., 1934.

Couvares, Francis G. *The Remaking of Pittsburgh: Class and Culture in an Industrializing City, 1877–1919.* Albany: State University of New York Press, 1984.

Cox, Kate Cabell. *Historical Sketch of Richmond's Oldest Chartered Charity Memorial Home for Girls.* Richmond: [n.p.], 1925.

Crawford, Mary Caroline. *The Romance of the American Theatre.* New York: Halcyon House, 1940.

Cunningham, Hugh. *Leisure in the Industrial Revolution.* London: St. Martin's Press, 1980.

Dabney, Virginius. *Richmond: The Story of a City.* Garden City, N.Y.: Doubleday & Co., 1976.

Davis, Richard Beale. *Francis Walker Gilmer: Life and Learning in Jefferson's Virginia.* Richmond: Dietz Press, 1939.

Davis, Susan G. *Parades and Power: Street Theatre in Nineteenth-Century Philadelphia.* Philadelphia: Temple University Press, 1986.

Dawley, Alan, and Paul Faler. "Working Class Culture and Politics in the Industrial Revolution: Sources of Loyalism and Rebellion." *Journal of Social History* 9 (Summer 1976): 466–80.

DeGrazia, Sebastian. *Of Time, Work, and Leisure.* New York: Twentieth Century Fund, 1962.

Denney, Reuel. *The Astonished Muse.* Chicago: University of Chicago Press, 1957.

Dizikes, John. *Sportsmen and Gamesmen.* Boston: Houghton Mifflin, 1981.

Dodd, Jill Siegel. "The Working Classes and the Temperance Movement in Ante-Bellum Boston." *Labor History* 19 (Fall 1978): 510–31.

Dormon, James H. *Theater in the Ante Bellum South, 1815–1861.* Chapel Hill: University of North Carolina Press, 1967.

———. "Thespis in Dixie: Professional Theater in Confederate Richmond." *Virginia Cavalcade* 28 (Summer 1978): 4–13.

Select Bibliography

Duke, Maurice, and Daniel P. Jordan, eds. *A Richmond Reader, 1733–1983*. Chapel Hill: University of North Carolina Press, 1983.

Dulles, Foster Rhea. *America Learns to Play: A History of Popular Recreation, 1607–1940*. New York: Peter Smith, 1952.

Dumazedier, Joffre. *Toward a Society of Leisure*. Trans. Stewart E. McClure. New York: Free Press, 1967.

Edwards, Harry. *Sociology of Sport*. Homewood, Ill.: Dorsey Press, 1973.

Edwards, Richard Henry. *Popular Amusements*. New York: Association Press, 1915.

Ezekiel, Herbert T., and Gaston Lichtenstein. *The History of the Jews of Richmond from 1769 to 1917*. Richmond: H. T. Ezekiel, 1917.

Fein, Isaac M. *The Making of an American Jewish Community: The History of Baltimore Jewry from 1773 to 1920*. Philadelphia: Jewish Publication Society of America, 1971.

Fiedler, Leslie. *Freaks: Myths and Images of the Secret Self*. New York: Simon and Schuster, 1978.

Fisk, George. *Leisure Spending-Behavior*. Philadelphia: University of Pennsylvania Press, 1963.

Gatewood, Joanne L., ed. "Richmond during the Virginia Constitutional Convention of 1829–1830; An Extract from the Diary of Thomas Green, October 1, 1829, to January 31, 1830." *Virginia Magazine of History and Biography* 84 (July 1976): 287–332.

Goheen, Peter G. "Industrialization and the Growth of Cities in Nineteenth-Century America." *American Studies* 14 (Spring 1973): 49–65.

Goldfield, David R. *Cotton Fields and Skyscrapers: Southern City and Region: 1607–1980*. Baton Rouge: Louisiana State University Press, 1982.

——. "Disease and Urban Image: Yellow Fever in Norfolk, 1855." *Virginia Cavalcade* 23 (Autumn 1973): 34–40.

——. *Urban Growth in the Age of Sectionalism: Virginia, 1847–1861*. Baton Rouge: Louisiana State University Press, 1977.

Goodspeed, David R. *Angling in America: Its Early History and Literature*. Boston: Houghton Mifflin, 1939.

Graham, Leroy. *Baltimore: The Nineteenth Century Black Capital*. Lanham, Md.: University Press of America, 1982.

Gray, David, and Donald A. Pelegrino, eds. *Reflections on the Recreation and Park Movement*. Dubuque, Iowa: W. C. Brown Co., 1973.

Gray, Ralph D., and Gerald E. Hartdagen. "A Glimpse of Baltimore Society in 1827: Letters by Henry D. Gilpin." *Maryland Historical Magazine* 59 (1964): 256–78.

Green, Arnold W. *Recreation, Leisure, and Politics*. New York: McGraw-Hill, 1964.

Green, Harvey. *The Light of the Home*. New York: Pantheon Books, 1983.

Griffen, Clyde, and Sally Griffen. *Natives and Newcomers: The Ordering of Opportunity in*

Mid-Nineteenth-Century Poughkeepsie. Cambridge and London: Harvard University Press, 1978.

Grimsted, David. *Melodrama Unveiled: American Theater and Culture, 1800–1850.* Chicago: University of Chicago Press, 1968.

Groves, Ernest R. *The American Woman: The Feminine Side of a Masculine Civilization.* Rept. New York: Arno Press, 1972.

Gruneau, Richard. *Class, Sports, and Social Development.* Amherst: University of Massachusetts Press, 1983.

Gutman, Herbert G. "Work, Culture, and Society in Industrializing America, 1815–1919." *American Historical Review* 78 (1973): 531–87.

Guttmann, Allen. *From Ritual to Record: The Nature of Modern Sports.* New York: Columbia University Press, 1978.

Hall, Clayton Colman. *Baltimore: Its History and Its People.* New York: Lewis Historical Pub. Co., 1912.

Hardy, Stephen. *How Boston Played: Sport, Recreation, and Community, 1865–1915.* Boston: Northeastern University Press, 1982.

——, and Alan G. Ingham. "Games, Structures, and Agency: Historians on the American Play Movement." *Journal of Social History* 17 (Fall 1983): 285–301.

Harris, Neil. *Humbug: The Art of P. T. Barnum.* Boston: Little, Brown, 1973.

Harrison, Brian. *Drink and the Victorians: The Temperance Question in England, 1815–1872.* Pittsburgh: University of Pittsburgh Press, 1971.

Hervey, John. *Racing in America, 1665–1865.* New York: Jockey Club, [1944].

Holliman, Jennie. *American Sports (1785–1835).* Durham, N.C.: Seeman Press, 1931.

Hornblow, Arthur. *A History of the Theatre in America.* 2 vols. Philadelphia: J. B. Lippincott Company, 1919.

Howe, Daniel Walker, ed. *Victorian America.* Philadelphia: University of Pennsylvania Press, 1976.

Hurlbut, Jesse Lyman. *The Story of Chautauqua.* New York: G. P. Putnam's sons, 1921.

Janssen, Frederick William. *A History of Amateur Athletics and Aquatics with the Records.* New York: Outing Club, 1887.

Janvier, Meredith. *Baltimore in the 80's and 90's.* Baltimore: H. G. Roebuck & Son, 1933.

——. *Baltimore Yesterdays.* Baltimore: H. G. Roebuck, 1937.

Johnson, David R. *Policing the Urban Underworld: The Impact of Crime on the Development of the American Police, 1800–1887.* Philadelphia: Temple University Press, 1979.

Jones, Gareth Stedman. "Class Expression versus Social Control? A Critique of Recent Trends in the Social History of 'Leisure.'" *History Workshop* 4 (Autumn 1977): 162–70.

Jones, Katherine M. *Ladies of Richmond, Confederate Capital*. Indianapolis: Bobbs-Merrill, 1962.

Kaplan, Max. *Leisure in America: A Social Inquiry*. New York: Wiley, 1960.

———. *Leisure: Theory and Policy*. New York: Wiley, 1975.

Kasson, John F. *Amusing the Million: Coney Island at the Turn of the Century*. New York: Hill & Wang, 1978.

———. *Civilizing the Machine: Technology and Republican Values in America, 1776–1900*. New York: Grossman Publishers, 1976.

Kett, Joseph F. *Rites of Passage: Adolescence in America 1790 to the Present*. New York: Basic Books, 1977.

Kirsch, George. "American Cricket." *Journal of Sport History* 2 (Spring 1984): 28–58.

Kraus, Richard. *Recreation and Leisure in Modern Society*. New York: Appleton-Century-Crofts, 1971.

Krout, John Allen. *The Origins of Prohibition*. New York: Alfred A. Knopf, 1925.

Laurie, Bruce. "'Nothing on Compulsion': Life Styles of Philadelphia Artisans, 1820–1850." *Labor History* 15 (Summer 1974): 337–66.

———. *Working People of Philadelphia, 1800–1850*. Philadelphia: Temple University Press, 1980.

Lebergott, Stanley. *The Americans: An Economic Record*. New York: W. W. Norton, 1984.

———. *Manpower in Economic Growth: An American Record since 1800*. New York: McGraw Hill, 1964.

Lebsock, Suzanne. *The Free Women of Petersburg: Status and Culture in a Southern Town, 1784–1860*. New York: W. W. Norton, 1984.

Lee, Richard M. *General Lee's City: An Illustrated Guide to the Historic Sites of Confederate Richmond*. McLean, Va.: EPM Publications, 1987.

Loy, John W., Jr., and Gerald S. Kenyon, eds. *Sport, Culture, and Society: A Reader on the Sociology of Sport*. New York: Macmillan, 1969.

Lucas, John A., and Ronald A. Smith. *Saga of American Sport*. Philadelphia: Lea & Febiger, 1978.

Lundberg, George Andrew, Mirra Komarovsky, and Mary Alice McInery. *Leisure: A Suburban Study*. New York: Columbia University Press, 1934.

Lutz, Earle. *A Richmond Album: A Pictorial Chronicle of an Historic City's Outstanding Events and Places*. Richmond: Garrett & Massie, 1937.

McCauley, Lois B. *Maryland Historical Prints, 1752 to 1889: A Selection from the Robert G. Merrick Collection, Maryland Historical Society, and Other Maryland Collections*. Baltimore: Maryland Historical Society, 1975.

Malcolmson, Robert W. *Popular Recreations in English Society, 1700–1850*. Cambridge: Cambridge University Press, 1973.

Manchester, Herbert. *Four Centuries of Sport in America, 1490–1890*. New York: Derrydale Press, 1931.

Select Bibliography

Mannheim, Karl. *Freedom, Power, and Democratic Planning*. New York: Routledge & K. Paul, 1950.

Meier, Hugo A. "Technology and Democracy, 1800–1860." *Mississippi Valley Historical Review* 43 (1957): 618–40.

Meredith, Henry Charles, comp. *A History of the Norfolk German Club, 1868–1960*. [Norfolk?], 1961.

Minnigerode, Meade. *The Fabulous Forties, 1840–1850*. New York: G. P. Putnam's Sons, 1924.

Mitchell, Mary H. *Hollywood Cemetery: The History of a Southern Shrine*. Richmond: Virginia State Library, 1985.

Mohl, Raymond A. "Poverty, Pauperism, and Social Order in the Preindustrial American City, 1780–1840." *Social Science Quarterly* 52 (March 1972): 934–48.

Montgomery, David. "The Working Class of the Preindustrial American City, 1780–1830." *Labor History* 9 (1968): 1–22.

Morrison, Andrew, ed. *The City on the James*. Richmond: G. W. Engelhardt, 1893.

Mrozek, Donald J. *Sport and American Mentality, 1880–1910*. Knoxville: University of Tennessee Press, 1983.

Neulinger, John, and Miranda Breit. "Attitude Dimensions of Leisure." *Journal of Leisure Research* 1 (1969): 255–61.

Norfolk Advertising Board, Inc. *Through the Years in Norfolk*. Portsmouth, Va.: Printcraft Press, 1937.

Norvell, Watkins. *Richmond, Virginia: Colonial Revolutionary, and Confederate, and the Present, 1896*. Richmond: E. B. Brown, 1896.

Nowitzky, George I. *Norfolk: The Marine Metropolis of Virginia*. Norfolk: G. I. Nowitzky, 1888.

O'Brien, John T. "Factory, Church, and Community: Blacks in Antebellum Richmond." *Journal of Southern History* 44 (Nov. 1978): 509–36.

Olson, Sherry H. *Baltimore: The Building of an American City*. Baltimore: Johns Hopkins University Press, 1980.

Owens, Hamilton. *Baltimore on the Chesapeake*. Garden City, N.Y.: Doubleday, Doran & Company, 1941.

Pearson, C. C., and J. Edwin Hendricks. *Liquor and Anti-Liquor in Virginia, 1619–1919*. Durham, N.C.: Duke University Press, 1967.

Pease, William H. and Jane H. *The Web of Progress: Private Values and Public Styles in Boston and Charleston, 1828–1843*. New York: Oxford University Press, 1985.

Peiss, Kathy. *Cheap Amusements: Working Women and Amusements in Turn-of-the-Century New York*. Philadelphia: Temple University Press, 1986.

Pollard, Julia Cuthbert. *Richmond's Story*. Richmond: Richmond Public Schools, 1954.

Rachleff, Peter J. *Black Labor in the South: Richmond, Virginia, 1865–1890*. Philadelphia: Temple University Press, 1984.

Select Bibliography

Rader, Benjamin G. *American Sports: From the Age of Folk Games to the Age of Spectators.* Englewood Cliffs, N.J.: Prentice-Hall, 1983.

Redlich, Fritz. "Leisure-Time Activities: A Historical, Sociological, and Economic Analysis." *Explorations in Entrepreneurial History,* 2d ser., 3 (Fall 1965): 3–24.

Reniers, Perceval. *The Springs of Virginia: Life, Love, and Death at the Waters, 1775–1900.* Chapel Hill: University of North Carolina Press, 1941.

Richmond, Capital of Virginia. [Richmond]: Whittet & Shepperson, 1938.

Riesman, David, and Reuel Denney. "Football in America: A Study in Culture Diffusion." *American Quarterly* 3 (1951): 309–25.

Riess, Steven A. *The American Sporting Experience: A Historical Anthology of Sport in America.* New York: Leisure Press, 1984.

Roberts, John, Malcolm J. Arth, and Robert R. Bush. "Games in Culture." *American Anthropologist* 61 (Aug. 1959): 597–605.

Rodgers, Daniel T. *The Work Ethic in Industrial America 1850–1920.* Chicago: University of Chicago Press, 1978.

Rosenzweig, Roy. *Eight Hours for What We Will: Workers and Leisure in an Industrial City, 1870–1920.* Cambridge: Cambridge University Press, 1983.

Ross, Steven J. *Workers on the Edge: Work, Leisure, and Politics in Industrializing Cincinnati, 1788–1890.* New York: Columbia University Press, 1985.

Rukert, Norman G. *Federal Hill: A Baltimore National Historic District.* Baltimore: Bodine & Associates, 1980.

Sage, George H. *Sport and American Society: Selected Readings.* Reading, Mass.: Addison-Wesley, 1974.

Sandiford, Keith A. P. "The Victorians at Play: Problems in Historiographical Methodology." *Journal of Social History* 15 (Winter 1981): 271–78.

Schlesinger, Arthur Meier. *The Rise of the City, 1878–1898.* New York: Macmillan Company, 1933.

Scott, Anne Firor. *The Southern Lady: From Pedestal to Politics, 1830–1930.* Chicago: University of Chicago Press, 1970.

Seeger, Charles. "Music and Class Structure in the United States." *American Quarterly* 9 (1957): 281–94.

Semmes, Raphael. *Baltimore as Seen by Visitors, 1783–1860.* Baltimore: Maryland Historical Society, 1953.

Shepherd, H. E., ed. *History of Baltimore, Maryland from Its Founding as a Town to the Current Year, 1729–1898.* Uniontown, Pa.: S. B. Nelson, 1898.

Shockley, Martin Staples. *The Richmond Stage, 1784–1812.* Charlottesville: University Press of Virginia, 1977.

Siossat, Annie Leakin. *Old Baltimore.* New York: Macmillan Co., 1931.

Snow, Robert E., and David E. Wright. "Coney Island: A Case Study in Popular Culture and Technical Change." *Journal of Popular Culture* 9 (Spring 1976): 960–75.

Somers, Dale A. "The Leisure Revolution: Recreation in the American City, 1820–1920." *Journal of Popular Culture* 5 (Summer 1971): 125–47.

———. *The Rise of Sports in New Orleans, 1850–1900.* Baton Rouge: Louisiana State University Press, 1972.

Squires, W. H. T. *Historical Norfolk, 1636 to 1936,* Book 1 of *Through the Years in Norfolk.* Portsmouth, Va.: Printcraft Press, 1937.

Stanard, Mary Newton. *Richmond: Its People and Its Story.* Philadelphia: J. B. Lippincott Company, 1923.

Steiner, Jesse Frederick. *Americans at Play: Recent Trends in Recreation and Leisure Time Activities.* New York: McGraw Hill, 1933.

Stick, David. *The Outer Banks of North Carolina.* Chapel Hill: University of North Carolina Press, 1958.

Sutherland, Willard C. "A Philosophy of Leisure." *Annals of the American Academy of Political and Social Science* 313 (Sept. 1957): 1–3.

Sutton, Robert P. "Nostalgia, Pessimism, and Malaise: The Doomed Aristocrat in Late-Jeffersonian Virginia." *Virginia Magazine of History and Biography* 76 (Jan. 1968): 41–55.

Taubman, Howard. *The Making of the American Theatre.* New York: Coward McCann, 1965.

Theodore, Terry. "The Confederate Theatre: Theatre Personalities and Practices during the Confederacy." *Lincoln Herald* 76 (Winter 1974): 187–95.

———. "The Confederate Theatre: The Confederate Drama." *Lincoln Herald* 77 (Spring 1975): 33–41.

———. "The Confederate Theatre in the Deep South." *Lincoln Herald* 77 (Summer 1975): 102–14.

———. "The Confederate Theatre: Richmond, Theatre Capital of the Confederacy." *Lincoln Herald* 77 (Fall 1975): 158–67.

Thompson, E. P. "Time, Work-Discipline, and Industrial Capitalism." *Past and Present* 38 (Dec. 1967): 56–97.

Toll, Robert C. *Blacking Up: The Minstrel Show in Nineteenth-Century America.* New York: Oxford University Press, 1974.

Tucker, George H. *Norfolk Highlights, 1584–1881.* Norfolk: Norfolk Historical Society, 1972.

Tyler-McGraw, Marie, and Gregg D. Kimball. *In Bondage and Freedom: Antebellum Black Life in Richmond, Virginia.* Richmond: Valentine Museum, 1988.

Veblen, Thorstein. *The Theory of the Leisure Class.* Rept. New York: Modern Library, 1934.

Vexler, Robert I., comp. and ed. *Baltimore: A Chronological and Documentary History.* Dobbs Ferry, N.Y.: Oceana Publications, 1975.

Voigt, David Quentin. *American Baseball: From Gentleman's Sport to the Commissioner System.* Norman: University of Oklahoma Press, 1966.

Select Bibliography

Wade, Richard C. *Slavery in the Cities*. New York: Oxford University Press, 1964.

Wallace, Irving. *The Fabulous Showman: The Life and Times of P. T. Barnum*. New York: Alfred A. Knopf, 1959.

Walvin, James. *Leisure and Society, 1830–1950*. London: Longman, 1978.

Ward, Harry M. *Richmond: An Illustrated History*. Northridge, Calif.: Windsor Publications, 1985.

Weddell, Alexander Wilbourne. *Richmond, Virginia, in Old Prints, 1737–1887*. Richmond: Johnson Publishing Co., 1932.

Wehrman, Ben. "Ocean View Marks Its 100 Years as a Resort." *Commonwealth* 21 (July 1954): 19–20.

Werner, M. R. *Barnum*. New York: Harcourt, Brace, 1923.

Wertenbaker, Thomas Jefferson. *Norfolk: Historic Southern Port*. Durham, N.C.: Duke University Press, 1931.

West, Mark Irwin. "A Spectrum of Spectators: Circus Audiences in Nineteenth-Century America." *Journal of Social History* 15 (Winter 1981): 265–70.

White, R. Clyde. "Social Class Differences in the Uses of Leisure." *American Journal of Sociology* 61 (Sept. 1955): 145–50.

Wilentz, Sean. *Chants Democratic: New York City and the Rise of the American Working Class, 1788–1850*. New York: Oxford University Press.

Wilmeth, Don B., ed. *American and English Popular Entertainment: A Guide to Information Sources*. Detroit: Gale Research Co., 1980.

Wittke, Carl. *Tambo and Bones*. Durham, N.C.: Duke University Press, 1930.

Yeo, Eileen, and Stephen Yeo. *Popular Culture and Class Conflict, 1590–1914: Explorations in the History of Labor and Leisure*. Atlantic Highlands, N.J.: Humanities Press, 1981.

Yoder, Paton. "The American Inn, 1775–1850: Melting Pot or Stewing Kettle?" *Indiana Magazine of History* 59 (1963): 135–51.

——. "Private Hospitality in the South, 1775–1850." *Mississippi Valley Historical Review* 47 (1960): 419–33.

Secondary Sources: Theses and Dissertations

Adelman, Melvin Leonard. "The Development of Modern Athletics: Sport in New York City, 1820–1870." Ph.D. diss., University of Illinois at Urbana-Champaign, 1980.

Bogger, Tommy Lee. "The Slave and Free Black Community in Norfolk, 1775–1865." Ph.D. diss., University of Virginia, 1976.

Bongiorno, Angela Catherine. "White Women and Work in Richmond, Virginia, 1870–1884." Master's thesis, University of Virginia, 1978.

Clark, Dennis Rankin. "Baltimore, 1729–1829: The Genesis of a Community." Ph.D. diss., Catholic University of America, 1976.

Muldrow, Blanche. "The American Theatre as Seen by British Travellers, 1790–1860." Ph.D. diss., University of Wisconsin, 1953.

Price, Margaret Nell. "The Development of Leadership by Southern Women through Clubs and Organizations." Master's thesis, University of North Carolina, 1945.

Shockley, Martin Staples. "A History of the Theatre in Richmond, Virginia, 1819–1838." Ph.D. diss., University of North Carolina, 1938.

Select Bibliography

Index

Index

Index

Index

Index